1969

THE CELIBATE CONDITION AND SEX

THE CELIBATE CONDITION AND SEX

MARC ORAISON

translated by Leonard Mayhew

SHEED AND WARD : NEW YORK

This book was originally published in French under the title Le Célibat.

Imprimatur: J. Ch. Gallissaires
Bordeaux, February 22, 1966

Library of Congress Catalog Card Number 67-21911

Manufactured in the United States of America

FOREWORD

DISCUSSING THE SUBJECT OF CELIBACY even nonacademically is more ticklish than might first appear. Since the middle of the last century science has vastly increased our knowledge of all aspects of sexuality and has, as a matter of fact, so broadened our vantage point and suggested so many new factors that our task has become ever more complicated.

Sexuality—and so, celibacy—is a problem with which we are all concerned directly since we are all, omitting the rare exceptions, male or female, and consequently we are celibates or not celibates. It is not possible to discuss sexuality or celibacy without some degree of personal involvement. From this there is no escape, for we are talking about our emotional and sexual life on its most radical and existential level; this must involve our entire personality as well as our deepest and, for the most part, unconscious choices. When we talk about celibacy, we are talking about ourselves, but without full realization. From Freud on, modern psychology has shown that when one talks about himself without this realization, he may well make embarrassing discoveries.

Naturally, whenever we speak, even trivially, we speak about ourselves. Clearly, however, I reveal much less and in a far less direct way if I am merely discoursing, for example, on the development of nuclear physics over the years. In such a case, the symbolic stratifications which separate my emotional experiences since birth from the language I use are so elaborate that I do not risk much self-revelation. When, on the other hand, I discuss celibacy, I am engaging those elements that condition the very core of my personality.

In other words, it is impossible to talk about celibacy impartially or objectively, since our emotional experiences are bound to intrude, even if unconsciously. The only thing we can do is to limit these distortions as far as possible. Thanks to psychoanalysis we know now that there is this inevitable intrusion, so we are less likely to fall into easy generalizations. Moreover, we can attempt to avoid emotional stances, which are only carefully disguised defensive or aggressive reactions, by reducing the discussion simply to a question of ecclesiastical or civil law.

Paradoxically, the recognition that one cannot be objective precisely allows us to be objective to a certain extent. Again this complicates our discussion.

To get an idea of how difficult the discussion is, we might take a look at the books on this subject written during the past century or so. Ignoring the tracts and pamphlets that are of no real interest, we note about twenty works of varying points of view. Since 1960 nothing has been catalogued at the *Bibliothèque Nationale* that deals directly with celibacy.

Of those which do treat this subject, we can point to a dramatic lack of background displayed by the authors.

They are ready to study celibacy without careful consideration of its real definition and implications. Some argue for or against celibacy so emotionally that one is forced to dismiss their work. Another smaller group pretends to a kind of emotional disinvolvement; this is particularly true of the historians of ecclesiastical celibacy. In connection with the latter, it is apparent that we must first of all reflect on certain newly discovered but nevertheless genuine aspects of the whole question of sexuality and celibacy. Such reflection is possible only by dint of modern psychology and contemporary philosophical insights.

CONTENTS

THE CELIBATE CONDITION AND SEX

I

GENERAL REFLECTIONS ON CELIBACY

1. THE HUMAN CONTEXT OF CELIBACY

OUR FIRST TASK is to determine as precisely as possible what it is we are discussing, even though this marks only the beginning of a reflective process which will attempt to probe much deeper. The dictionary is an obvious starting point. It provides a simple definition of celibacy: the state of one who is not married.

At first glance, there is nothing very new in that. Take a closer look, however. Celibacy is negatively defined by reference to *marriage*, not by reference to *actual cohabitation.* This is a major distinction.

We must then ascertain the precise definition of marriage. It is generally agreed that marriage is a social and juridical institution focused on sexuality both broadly and specifically, with allowance for extremely varied styles in different civilizations. A social institution surrounded with an entire complex of rites which are usually not directly sexual (monogamy being a separate question), marriage demands in some form the official presence of a personage who represents the pervading social organization. This individual links the sexually-bound couple with organized society.

For a marriage to take place there must be a man and

woman who agree to be joined together in the presence of someone who represents officially the human group to which they belong. In this way the group itself is present. The marriage is constituted by the presence of witnesses and especially of this privileged witness who is publicly charged with this role.

Marriage cannot take place between persons of the same sex because the reproductive nature of sexuality is of its essence. By the same token, there can be no marriage without the official presence of organized society. The insignia of the person who embodies this social context is required, whether it be the mayor's sash or the pastor's stole. In addition, in Western society any number of other signs of the marital consent are required–rings, special costumes, signing the register.

This is to speak of marriage simply phenomenologically, without considering the sacramental aspect of Christian marriage. This aspect transfers the same complex reality to the supernatural level in terms of the Mystical Body.

In monogamous marriage a man and woman pronounce a *word*, which binds them in the most all-embracing relationship possible, before a third party who is present precisely to hear it. This third party is actually the social organization which surrounds the couple. The marriage is far more than a sexual joining; it marks, as well, a new and unique relationship to society. First, the man and woman recognize each other as partners in life and fecundity. Secondly, they demand to be recognized as such by society and by the authority which represents society.

On the other hand, celibacy is the state of someone who does not ask society to recognize him as joined in a sexual union. Whether or not he is actually sexually involved, he is not *married* unless he pronounces the word of consent before others who hear it, deliberately relating himself to them also in a context clearly linked to social authority.

Great importance must be attached to this word of consent being *heard by the social third party*. This indicates a real socialization since it establishes a style of life in which each party clearly recognizes his position relative to others.

The sex act is perhaps the most social of all acts because it alone can produce a third person. The child is also sexed and will, in his turn, reproduce. In the space of a century generations come and go.

We are talking about human beings, who are specifically different from animals. The entire psycho-affective universe which precedes and underlies our consciousness comes into play. Human offspring do not grow to maturity like animals. On this central point Freud's discoveries revealed unsuspected insights. Only marriage, which furnishes a stable socialization of sexuality, can provide normal sexual fulfillment.

To consider only one side of the question, recall that according to these new discoveries an infant enjoys normal physical and psychological growth only if he lives in a climate of adequate affective security. For his first years this climate is directly created by the affective attitude of his mother and her own deep-down security. Her security is encouraged, to say the very least, if she knows that she is recognized as the mother of this particular man's child.

In all the complex and varied relationships of her concrete life, from the grocer to the Social Security office, she realizes that those around her recognize her stable and enduring status. Aside from clearly neurotic cases, for an adult to feel himself fully and personally recognized and to be able to enter easily into the framework of his life, he must have been raised by a mother who felt herself recognized as a wife. A woman's married name which might seem a mere administrative convenience is, on the contrary, of primary importance, as daily clinical experience attests.

The married name is not merely an external courtesy; it is a title and it is understood as such by the woman it designates and whom it helps to situate. Properly understood, this can be achieved only within society.

The creation of patterns by human society—patterns not previously and immutably determined by animal instinct—is complex. This problem is directly related to sexuality and consequently to the question of celibacy.

Most likely the primary consideration in human socialization is the prohibition of incest which Freud shows to be a basic imperative. The Oedipus crisis in the infant's primitive world means that the parent of the opposite sex is immediately sensed as sexually forbidden.

This prohibition is quickly extended to all those of the opposite sex. This becomes a primordial distinction in the human world surrounding the child: one does not have sexual relations with certain people. These people immediately assume a role and meaning as absolutely *other*.

Without pressing this line of reasoning too far, we may assert that it is here that the child begins to discover *persons*—sexually characterized certainly, but extending well beyond the sexual. This is the first distinction which elaborates truly intersubjective relationships in which *words* play a specific and fundamental role.

Society does not create this prohibition. Words first create the human relationships, and subsequently society conforms to this primitive prohibition. Social taboos follow in order to structure—or exacerbate—our anxiety or fear of breaking this basic prohibition.

Taken broadly as the elementary social organization, the family discovers its structure in this process. It is easy to see then that marriage—two persons' pledge of common life and of reproduction—necessarily implies a verbally expressed link with the human context in which they must live.

Celibacy must be considered in relation to all this. It is something quite distinct from systematic sexual continence. We can bring about sexual continence in animals quickly and once and for all, as we do with most city pets, whether or not they are castrated, clearly the most radical solution. Origen's error was sub-human in that he confused celibacy and castration.[1] It is impossible to conceive animals being in a celibate state. Words are specifically human. So marriage, the socialization of sex by a word, and celibacy, the nondeclaration of this word, are

[1] Origen, a Christian philosopher who lived and taught in Alexandria and Caesarea during the second century, castrated himself out of a misguided zeal for purity.

also specifically human. It is only a figure of speech to speak of an old "hermit" boar as a "bachelor."

Still on the level of phenomenological reflection we can now place the celibate in perspective: he is an individual who does not enter into the social interplay of sexuality. He may have positive reasons for deciding not to exercise his sexual powers. Or, he may exercise them in a more or less egocentric manner, closed in on himself, without participating in the general process of socialization. He may have sexual relations with one partner after another. He may even bind himself in a stable relationship by a word he speaks privately to his partner but is unwilling for others to hear and recognize. He rejects the crystallization of others' presence in the person of social authority. The social adjustment and maturity—a much-abused but still valuable word—of such a person is very open to question.

No lengthy argument is needed to demonstrate this thesis. The man who declares his love to a woman and chooses her for companion and sexual partner without wanting anyone to know it *officially* does not bind himself in the same way as if he proclaimed it to others and affirmed his freedom and involvement in society. By refusing to allow his word to be heard, he binds himself only halfway.

The reflections of a former juvenile delinquent who had a hard time adjusting to society were enlightening. He was in love, and he and his fiancée had every intention to be married legally. He was not religious, and I did not think he would even dream of a Church wedding. That was exactly what he asked for, however, and his reason surprised me at first: "Only in the presence of the priest will I feel that I have bound myself to her freely and personally before someone."

In his mind civil marriage was only an administrative formality. He wanted more, even though his profound intuition was unclearly formulated. He demanded that the privileged word he was to address to his wife be heard and recognized by someone whom he considered dependable—a trustworthy witness. He wanted to feel that he was recognized in his sexual commitment and to obtain a kind of guarantee, an official promise that would help him move toward the full realization of the state of life he was taking on.

Now we can define celibacy more precisely: it is the attitude of one who does not bind himself in a socialized sexual relationship which is confirmed by a word pronounced simultaneously to his partner and to the society that witnesses it.

Several possibilities can be imagined. An individual may marry, according to our definition of marriage, but maintain sexual continence. This is not unheard of, although it is usually a pathological situation. Sometimes such a marriage may be only a legal fiction which allows the two partners to achieve legal or psychological autonomy from their parents. The Church does not recognize this as a complete marriage.

If the parties can prove they have not had sexual relations and if there is an important reason, the marriage can be broken and they become single again. If the verbal contract, on the other hand, has been consummated by sexual relations, no human power can do anything about it. This helps to underline to what a degree, at least implicitly, the Church understands that the sexual relationship represents a transcendental value.

An individual may not marry but may live instead in an enduring sexual union–concubinage. There are situations of this kind which are stable, even definitive, but they are not marriages because the *word* of commitment is merely implicit and the parties have not wished it to be heard. This choice may reveal a subsocial, or even antisocial, attitude. In any case, it poses a problem because both juridically and on *the level of at least subconscious experience* such persons remain single.

I knew a respectable man who lived in concubinage for twenty years and refused to marry because he refused to be heard by the official witness of a republic which had imprisoned Marshal Pétain. He and his wife were deeply religious. However, he could not marry in the Church because in France one has to be previously married in a civil ceremony. After twenty years, the woman was able to patiently lead this typical rigidist neurotic out of this strange repulsion.

An individual may be neither married nor involved in an enduring concubinage but run through one affair after another. This attitude is no longer only sub- or anti-social. It poses a real question about the balance of the personality since celibacy and promiscuity, affective as well as physical, are combined.

A curious book by Octave Uzenne, which appeared in

1912, was entitled *Celibacy and Love, A Treatise on the Emotional Life and Female Direction.* It is a kind of apologia for celibacy but full of irony and harboring ill-concealed bitterness. The typical lover—the typical bachelor, according to the author—is described as egocentric and somewhat paranoic. It relates a fascinating "bachelor's dialogue" taken from Chamfort:

"Will you marry?"
"No."
"Why?"
"Because I would be unhappy."
"Why would you be unhappy?"
"Because I would be jealous."
"Why would you be jealous?"
"Because I would be deceived."
"Why would you be deceived?"
"Because I would deserve it."
"Why would you deserve it?"
"Because I had married."

This admirable tautology camouflages the very deep and terrible anguish of a man who sees himself "deceived in advance," that is, as essentially incapable of being loved.

Finally, an individual may be single, not living in concubinage, and continent. Contrary to contemporary prejudice, this is not a fantastic situation and may be widely observed. It is here that the psychological ambivalence of celibacy is seen. It may be, as clinical experience shows, either an expression of repression and neurosis or, quite the opposite, the realization of a deep balance and affective maturity.

What complicates everything is there can also be individuals who marry in the true sense of the word and accept, according to their ability, the meaning of their *word* but who are more or less immature psychologically. They are incapable of *living* in a postive way with a partner of the opposite sex, even though they are quite capable of sexual relations. In one degree or another this is fairly widespread.

2. THE FACT AND THE MEANING

IN THE LIGHT of the modern sciences concerned with man and without any reference to moral concerns, we see in marriage, with its social implications, a truly intersubjective sexual union as the achieved and spontaneous fulfillment of affective evolution. It represents at least a *psychological possibility* and a profound aspiration.

We must weigh our words. We say "the achieved and spontaneous fulfillment . . . at least a psychological possibility." We avoid the word "normal" which would cause confusion by oversimplification. "Normal" means to conform to a norm, a law. Medically speaking, it is normal that the evolution of the embryo and fetus should end in the birth of a normally constituted child who lacks nothing—in the biological sense—that nature produces when unimpeded. Psycho-affective sexuality also normally conforms to the individual's anatomic-physiological make-up, that is, his sex, and should ultimately be realized in a socio-sexual relationship. The usually very primitive development toward homosexuality, or what are called sexual perversions,[1] is in this sense abnormal.

[1] This term is taken in a clinical, not moral, sense.

But, if it is normal that a human being desire and be able to marry—in the full sense of the word—it is not normal that he be obliged to do so. Whether a normally developed individual chooses to marry or not goes beyond any medically conceived norm and reaches the level of what is gratuitous, that is, free. At least this is what clinical experience suggests. We find many married couples who don't get along and are pathological and many celibates who get along fine and are normal. We can, as well, find abnormal celibates and normal married couples.[2]

If we consider ideal married life, which, at the very least, demands an enduring confrontation which offers both partners self-fulfillment in the union, we must take for granted that this success presumes that each has the psychological capacity for a sexually-based relationship.[3] Each partner must be prepared to live with someone else who is radically different, sexually opposite. He must be ready to accept this *otherness*, this uniqueness of the other party as a *subject*. He must be ready to hear and respond "yes" or "no" to the implicit and constant demand of his partner without feeling threatened in his own affective identity and basic security. Each must be able to take the other into account without his own sense of worth being diminished.

The presence of another person within one's world is essentially a demand. Without probing its obscure roots,

[2] Generally more common than we suppose because nobody pays attention to "normal" married couples.

[3] As we shall see, in order to be successful positive celibacy demands this same capacity.

as psychoanalysis has revealed them, the basic demand is that one be accepted by the person to whom he presents himself in his singular existence, outlook, style—in short, personality. It means being recognized as "I" with all that that value implies. This is the thread from which the fabric of every dialogue is woven.

It may be easy for a man to understand and accept this demand from another man, even a rival. However, modern psychology has shown that it is an entirely different case between man and woman. The demand in this case is radically different, truly *other*. Modern discoveries of the human personality demonstrate this essential difference as a repercussion of sexual differentiation.

Woman's instinctive "presence to the world" is radically different from man's, even though for both this presence means a psychological consciousness based on affectivity. Freud's discoveries and the resultant understanding of the affective development of children demonstrate that it could not be otherwise and point out the fundamental biopsychical roots of sexual difference.

Without going into the details of this research, it is sufficient to know that the subjective structuring of the child's personality in relationship to others in primordially conditioned by whether or not there is present a visible and examinable sexual organ. Granted sufficiently normal environmental conditions, the infinitely complex interplay of the child's discoveries, anxieties, and conquered fears leads him to form what is at first an obscure and unconscious self-image which relates to this basic and discernible biological fact.

It is perfectly normal for a man to place himself instinctively in the world as one who can examine, know, and classify everything. He is the one to take the initiative, to seek to penetrate, to act, and to destroy whatever resists him. For a woman, it is normal to conceive of herself as one who senses more than she sees, who perceives things interiorly, who acts by receiving, which to men, at least, seems an irrational process. She is the one who creates mysteriously within herself. If everything always went according to plan, each would instinctively sense his complementarity.

Many of a child's affective crises that end up more or less resolved focus precisely on this point of possession or loss of this primordial sexual symbol.[4] As a result, dialogue between the sexes—in the broadest sense and not only in intercourse—is perpetually described by dialectic and tension. A normal heterosexual union means precisely the indefinitely repeated surpassing and resolving of this dialectic and tension.

From this perspective it is understandable that sexual relations are quite insufficient to establish a stable relationship between a man and woman, unless they are the privileged and intense expression of a broader and continuing exchange. More bluntly, it is easy for a man to sleep with a woman, but this is not going to have much meaning for either of them unless he is capable of *living* with her. This demands a good deal more from the viewpoint of escaping from narcissism.

[4] This is the infinitely complex problem that we term "castration anxiety."

Many couples get along fairly well with each other on the basis of a kind of negotiated compromise. Desire for the sexual act per se often becomes dominant to the degree that a broader sexual relationship has not been established. The greater capacity an individual has for broadly based sexual relationships, the less likely it is that his sexual drives will get beyond his control. This conclusion is attested by clinical psychology.[5] In pathological relationships on the other hand, where there is no undisturbed sexual dialectic, sexual relations can have many obscure meanings for both partners and will be no help at all to them.

Let us return now to celibacy which may exist whether or not the subject remains continent. Celibacy is an observable fact and the object of medico-psychological observation. Physicians and psychologists will see this phenomenon in much more depth because of their professional experience. They will immediately observe that celibacy occurs frequently and, secondly, that it is extremely diversified.

The fact that there are continent celibates who live satisfactory lives and humanly fulfill themselves immediately poses a central problem: such a life is possible. Even if there were only one case out of 10,000 people, the problem would still remain. On this point among others, the Kinsey Report has presented considerable matter for thought. Fortunately it reversed a number of ideas we

[5] We exclude cases of sexual repression which are almost always accompanied by disturbances affecting all sexually-based relationships.

took for granted. It gives two testimonies of interest to us which mark the extremes of male sexual behavior.

The first respondent to the anonymous inquiry states that he practices coitus five or six times a day. The second, who lives an intense intellectual and social life, mentions only two or three nocturnal ejaculations in a year. This directly contradicts the stubborn popular prejudice that a man's sexual activity is aroused by a constraining physiological rhythm similar to bodily excretions. We now know that the sexual physiology of men shows just the contrary, that there is no precise physiological rhythm of this kind. Sexual excitement always has a psychic point of departure, conscious or not. The formation of the sperm is only the final consequence of this excitement when it has been carried to the intensity of orgasm.

In women, of course, there is the physiological rhythm of ovulation which begins at puberty and ceases at menopause, and thus is clearly a temporary phenomenon. This cycle only slightly affects spontaneous behavior except for occasional cases of complicated psychosomatic disturbance. It has nothing in common with the intensity of the female animal's heat. Endocrinologists assert that, even regarding hormonal physiology, we cannot draw inferences regarding what takes place in humans from what we observe in animals. We have to deal with something new, that is, psychic life.

Even in animals, sexual continence is physiologically possible. We can definitively prevent a cat or bitch from having sexual relations—merely by penning them during their periods of heat—without injuring their health or shortening their life. The animal will be disturbed during its period of heat but afterward will return to its normal habits.

It is a confusing fact of everyday observation that sexual activity is not indispensable to the individual living organism in order that it might maintain its existence and biological balance. The observable intensity of the sexual urge contrasts strikingly with the fact that physiological sex is an optional biological activity for the individual. We can clarify this a little by some elementary reflection on what we call instinct, for lack of a better name.

Every living organism appears to be a complex of needs. Life is essentially characterized by the dynamic autonomy of its formation and existence. Unlike inert matter, a living being possesses the need and potential to form itself and to maintain its existence in the mature form it achieves. On the level of life the relationship to environment becomes dynamic, individual–*active*. We refer to these phenomena as *natural needs* because, in the observable world, they appear only on the level of life. An amethyst, once it is formed by a complex geological process, persists passively in its form as long as nothing external intervenes. A seed of grain, however, becomes wheat only through a truly mysterious, individual, and intrinsic activity.

Examining the total phenomenon of life we discover these needs to be of two analogous yet very different types. The first can be described as the individual's need to attain his own perfect morphology—to be adult or mature. This need may remain dormant for a long time, as in the case of a vegetative seed, or may express itself without the possibility of delay, as the eggs of an animal, for example. This is the *need to be*, and to be in the fulness of one's specific form. There is a need to maintain this existence by active exchange with the environment and to defend it against external threats by organizing permanent and reflex defenses which are sometimes surprising in their precision and effectiveness.

The second natural need is like the first, that is, the need to reach and maintain maximum existence, but conceived now in terms of the *species*, the group of individuals of like structure. According to modern biology the aging and death of cells is a normal life process. The species as such can persist only if the individuals which make it up reproduce themselves in new individuals. This is the very nature of life from its first appearance in the original single-celled organism. The species struggles for its existence by the reproduction of individuals whose existence is necessarily transitory. These needs express themselves in the activity and behavior of individuals. To put it more succinctly, we may say that instinct leads the individual to act out of need.

The instincts of aggression—in the etymological sense of the term, to "move toward" maximum being—correspond to the first order of needs. It is clear that this group of instincts directly concerns the individual and tends to insure his existence. When it becomes impossible for the individual to exercise these instincts, so that he can no longer satisfy his constitutive needs, he is in danger of premature death. Hunger, thirst, the need for shelter, self-defense, etc. are instincts of this type.

The second group of instincts is a different matter. These do not insure the individual's needs but, through him, serve the needs of the species. These are the instincts of reproduction, that is, of sexuality. Sexuality is established very early in the hierarchy of living beings, even in some protozoa. Even though the individual experiences these instincts most profoundly, they do not seek to insure his existence—which is insured by other means—but that of the species. An individual of the species may fail to exercise his sexual instincts and may not satisfy his periodic or continuous sexual needs without any threat of death or even serious permanent trouble to his own biological structure and life. In relation to the maintenance of his own existence, sex is literally a *marginal* biological activity.

Biologically speaking, there is no difference when we reach the special level of this "new" living being, man. From the outset, however, his instincts have only feeble influence on the precise and immediate adaptation of his behavior. Starting with the obscure world of his earliest experiences and going all the way to the level of clear consciousness, there is elaborated in place of instinct a pattern of personal auto-regulation rediscovered by and for each individual out of his strictly singular prehistory and history. This introduces the possibility of basic conflict between biological forces and unformed primitive instincts.

On the level of the unconscious motivations behind the nonexercise of sexuality, there *can* be disturbances, what we call repressions or neuroses, keeping in mind that we are talking about *unconscious* processes. Even if certain neurotic personal situations may end in suicide, which is a *specifically human* act, the biological disturbances resulting from nonexercise of sexuality remain as negligible for humans as for animals. If health problems do result, they grow out of the neurosis. In such cases it is not exaggerated to say that both the continence and the health problem are equally symptomatic of a more profound psychic disorder. In general, this represents the present outlook of psychosomatic medicine.

The existential situation of celibacy, continent or not, is a fact which does not raise any biological problems. It is a *human* fact. And, it is a fact which is situated in a *negation:* not pronouncing the word of sexual union before the social witness with all that entails in terms of commitment.

On reflection this fact seems profoundly strange. It seems to be natural—in the sense of what is spontaneous and biologically possible—and yet at the same time to run counter to the potent and fundamental attraction which is characteristic of sexuality. What significance can it have in relation to the meaning of sexuality?

A "negation." Even though every comparison is by definition unsatisfactory, it may be necessary to use one here. A native of New York is able *not* to go to San Francisco for one of several reasons: he may *not* be able to leave New York . . . he may *not* like San Francisco . . . he may *prefer* Los Angeles—in this last case he is capable both of leaving New York and of feeling sympathetic toward San Francisco.

A human being may simply *not* marry. Or because sexual activity is in a sense optional, he may desire some particular form of fulfillment which is more important to him than the fulfillment of marriage. The first type of celibacy is negative; the second, positive. In the world of real people a concrete problem may arise from the possibility of alibis—positive conscious motivations intended to justify and camouflage the really decisive negative and unconscious motives. In another section we shall pursue this viewpoint in what we shall call the clinical study of celibacy.

Whether it is positive or negative, the fact of celibacy introduces a crucial question about the value and importance of a human being's sexual realization. As long as celibacy exists in the world and is not absolutely exceptional, we must admit that sexual realization through a fully socialized heterosexual union is not necessarily the ultimate end of every person's fulfillment. Love, as currently understood, even considered in its ultimate meaning in a successful marriage, is neither the last word nor the ultimate aim of human aspirations. If we do not admit this, positive celibacy would be impossible and negative celibacy would always end in suicide.

This is not the least striking aspect of the relativity of love and sexual need. If sexual realization in the socialized union of man and woman may cause such fear on the most unconscious level that some people are enabled to remain celibate or if there exist poles of affective and spiritual interest which can transcend such realization, it is because we are dealing with a profoundly ambivalent existential commitment marked simultaneously by primordial importance and radical insufficiency. The *fact* of celibacy, whatever it may mean, casts light on the insoluble mystery of human sexuality.

There is no intention here of minimizing the complex reality of sex. Still less do I intend to minimize the value derived from its most complete realization in marriage for fulfillment on every level including the most spiritual. On first examination the love of a man and woman fully articulated within society is, even in its strictly physical expression, certainly the most beautiful human achievement. At the same time, even in its very success it appears relative and insufficient in the final analysis. The success of such love is much more frequent than is commonly supposed. Relative as this success may be, it presents this paradoxical aspect: it introduces individuals to the *positive* discovery of relationships which tend toward the infinite and by this very fact makes them realize that the infinite is beyond their reach.

Human love is like the whole human condition. Absolute happiness does not exist in time—I was going to say "by definition"—since its nature is "to be pursued." People loftily declare themselves "perfectly happy." If it were totally true, they would not feel the need to say so or hear themselves say so.

If we view this fact in the light of the Judaeo-Christian revelation, we find a curious reconcilation. Whether one accepts it or not, this revelation fully developed ends with the idea that God is love and that he is one because he is three. The "number of love" is three. The mark of human reality, however, is the "number" two: differentiation into two sexes. To their credit, Freud and his successors brought to light this fundamental conditioning of consciousness even in its most obscure roots. The essential rhythm of sexuality is the "two" tending toward the "one" through the appearance of a third, the offspring. But the "third person" who appears can only be a man or a woman. Sexuality is so designed that it cannot transcend the "two."

But its very dynamism—a divine creation—nevertheless seeks to transcend it in the direction of the *three in one.* Sexuality, which implies differentiation into two individuals, imitates the dynamism of the relationship of love as it exists transcendentally in God. It falls back upon itself in an ambivalent illusion which is experienced in the most subtle and profound human suffering. What is the secret of this fundamental mystery of human love—more real and less explorable than any human being before the advent of modern science could have realized?

A successful marriage is certainly the deepest manifestation of unity between two persons. Everyday language expresses it well: "they really are only one person"—"the Joneses or the Smiths are a real team, really inseparable." The internal logic of human speech expresses it even more basically: this man and this woman, that is, two persons, form one couple, that is, a *unity.*

Alphonse Daudet remarks that in families who really share things with each other, the husband and wife end by looking alike! Genesis likewise says it: "they shall be two in one flesh." This may be the strongest expression of the unity of the human couple.

This unity is never fully and definitively achieved. It is never acquired once and for all in *absolute* transparency toward each other, in *total* exchange of what Paul Claudel calls "the soul" in the dialogue of Prouheze and Camille in *The Satin Slipper*. There is always something incommunicable, some "secret," which cannot be expressed and communicated to the other person.

Even in the positive and profound love of deeply united couples there persists a muffled and insoluble nostalgia, a subtle but real suffering. *Without being ever resolved*, this can progressively contribute to the oneness they seek. Once again, the intense logic of human speech expresses this impossibility and this ambivalence. We say "Mr. and Mrs. So-and-so"—"they are very close"—"what an ideal couple: he has this quality, she has the other."

On the administrative level the family record translates the impossibility of expressing ideal unity except by separating family names—which recalls everything that preceded their meeting without being able to absorb or resolve the distinction.

Nevertheless this total unity, in which each becomes more himself as he succeeds in giving himself to the other, remains the goal. The ultimate search of all life leads toward it in spite of the perpetual conflict of ambivalence. Like a shipwrecked man swimming toward a shore he sees but never reaches, the most successful human love tends toward the total unity it sees as its end but cannot achieve. The sexual act is undoubtedly the situation in which this ambivalence is most intensely expressed.

The insoluble dialectic of time and love is most manifest on the level of sexual union. The contradiction between life and death appears most intense in terms of sexuality.

Taken as a biological whole, the sexual organization of the living word is oriented basically and exclusively to the indefinite preservation of the phenomenon of life. From its very emergence the biosphere defends itself by sexuality against disappearance. We cannot yet truly speak of time, because time means the subjective apprehension by human consciousness of this conflict. The conscious grasp of *experienced time* by an individual is always crucial because it means the discovery that the "I" is directly concerned with death. This is indisputably an aspect of the emotional awakening of adolescence.

While it is the area in which life expands, sexuality as a biological fact is also the revelation of individual death. When the scientist examines the hierarchy of beings, sexuality manifests itself as a distinct function on the same level where the evidence of distinct and individual mortality appears. Elementary monocellular beings like the amoeba are not sexed in any way; reproduction and expansion of the species are accomplished by scissiparity. At a certain moment of its development an amoeba separates into two new amoebas; the first individual element splits into two second elements. It does not endure in its own existence and structure independently of the reproductive process.

As soon as sexual organization appears, on the level of certain protozoa, everything changes. Two individuals, differently structured and with reciprocal complementarity in one detail of their make-up, come together, connect at precisely these points, and by that process bring into being subsequent individuals. In this activity and afterward they continue to exist with their own form and biological distinction. Only at this level do we observe the phenomenon of aging and death, the cessation of active exchange, and the decomposing of the organism into its chemical elements. The very word decomposition expresses what we are saying.

In other words, the biologist can discover this *normal* aspect of the life phenomenon—aging and death—only from the point where the living organism is at least elementarily sexed. Sexuality as such is a perfection of the individuation and permanence of life, pushed further and further in the higher animals. Simultaneously, it reveals individual mortality.

Human beings do not escape the fundamental laws of biology even though they have a new mode of presence in the world: differentiation and consciousness.

In order to clarify in depth the surprising fact of celibacy, it seemed necessary to bring out the profound ambivalence of sexuality in general and human sexuality in particular. Celibacy is properly a negative or positive noninvolvement in the complete realization of experienced sexuality.

II

CLINICAL STUDY OF NEGATIVE CELIBACY

3. NEGATIVE CELIBACY

CELIBACY DOES NOT EXIST. Celibates exist—human beings living in a situation whose various levels of significance we intend to explore. When we pass from theory to reflection on concrete situations, we come to grips with a practically insoluble difficulty inherent in every human situation. Every person lives in his own way and according to his own history. There is no possibility of valid generalities.

Nevertheless, we must try to clarify and organize our observations. We must discern differences or convergences which will enable us to describe the various forms of celibacy. It would be the greatest deception to imagine that we could in this way exhaust the question. This would be a failure to recognize the undefinable singularity of persons. It would be to force real individuals into preconceived categories and to deny the inexpressible and mysterious complexity of human reality.

It must be understood beforehand that our intention is to clarify the main ideas, not to establish narrow definitions. Any examples we use explicitly or implicitly will only be for illustration. The order is necessarily arbitrary. Indeed, it would be astonishing if it were not conditioned by the author's own emotional state. We must necessarily adopt a simple expositive style. We shall examine first what we call "negative" celibacy and different problems connected with it. Then we shall study "positive" celibacy. Finally we shall broach the delicate question of "institutional" celibacy.

By "negative celibacy" we mean situations which express an incompleteness or repression of sexual fulfillment. Such situations and the psychological problems which accompany them are infinitely varied.

Even people without training in clinical psychology can often discern that someone has a problem. Everyday language expresses it by nuances: we speak of "old bachelors"—a term which does not mean the same as "single persons." Sometimes we express particular astonishment that an individual is unmarried.

When modern psychology methodically examines such cases, we discern problems—sometimes cleverly concealed—concerned with relationships between the sexes. The psychological difficulty resides on the level of these generalized relationships much more than on the superficial and symptomatic level of sexual activity. However much the basic factors and surface characteristics vary, the root lies always in an incapacity to accept the public commitment of a stable sexual union.

The negative celibate cannot expose his emotional security as a *sexual* being to the social third party. This fear represents primitive experiences which he cannot sort out or suitably interpret. The threat he senses from affirming himself sexually to another is so great that he cannot face it. We must keep in mind that this emotional conflict takes place on the deepest, most obscure level of his unconscious mind.

NEGATIVE CELIBACY IN MEN

As we have pointed out, a child's physical sexual make-up plays a central role in his emotional development. The presence or absence of an external sexual organ conditions the image of his body with which the child begins, obscurely and intensely, to form an image of himself in relation to others—his parents. A man is one "who has. . . ." One of the central difficulties of development revolves around a fear of loss of virility—not in the sense of sexual potency but of the general value of being a man. This fear must be understood in the broadest, most symbolic, and most polymorphous sense possible.

We can give a few examples. We are frequently surprised at a man who lives with a woman faithfully for many years, has children, shows no desire to leave them, but still refuses to marry. All the arguments about legality, social advantages, legitimation of the children have no effect. They do not penetrate. We are tempted to say, "You live as if you were married. Why not go ahead?" He has no coherent or valid answer. To justify such a faithful but unofficial union, some men use the old saw about marriage killing love.

Why should marriage kill love? Because marriage means bringing in this third social witness invested with the authority to recognize the union. This is precisely what such a man cannot face. He can enter a satisfactory sexual union only on condition that it does not have to be recognized or placed in a social context. Some call this freedom without being able to see that they are prisoners of an obscure fear of allowing themselves to be recognized in a legitimate situation.

When we examine such paradoxical persons more closely we quickly discover that all their social relationships are disturbed: lack of real contact, timidity, instability, difficulty in getting along with others, antisocial feelings, secretiveness, little freedom or spontaneity. Relationships with professional superiors are usually tense and restricted. Such persons are considered "odd ducks" by colleagues and neighbors—hard to understand, subjects for gossip.

The underlying conditioning of such an attitude can be very varied. Such a person is still subject to fear of Oedipal guilt. He may have had an apparently normal childhood except for an authoritarian father who recognized his independence too late and incompletely.

If we follow the course of his relations with his father, we discover that he was never able to clear the rivalry crisis which would have given him identity. He detached himself from the early emotional bonds with his mother. He identified himself with his father in the essential direction of his sexual orientation but never enough to affirm it without the archaic and imaginary fear of paternal reaction. He may desire sexual union but only if his father does not know or, at least, if he does not have to tell him outright.

From the viewpoint of personality development, when a young man marries he implicitly says to his father, "My turn. I am your equal. I too have the right to be called a man." If, for one reason or another, relations with his father have been disturbed by primitive fears, there may be conflicts and wounds at the time of crossing the threshold of sexual maturity. This is not rare. But, when it is impossible for a son to cross this threshold, we have a *celibate* who may live in a stable sexual union but can never *declare it to authority*.

For another man the same situation may be the expression of a fear of being cornered. He feels unsure of himself when anybody is watching him. He feels free only when he is not being observed. This has to be understood as an immediate and frequently illogical emotional reaction. This other person whose observation paralyzes him may be imaginary and completely within himself—even subimaginary. At work he may be quite relaxed under the direction and supervision of his superior. Alone at home, however, panic will seize him at the thought of going out to buy a car. He may never summon up the strength to do it. If he does, it will become an adventure from which he cannot extricate himself. It will be too burdensome to bear.

This interior witness who watches him will make too great demands. In the eyes of this witness he is always inferior. Such a man may well seek the fulfillment of living with a woman but he will never dare face the gaze of this interior someone he cannot escape. He will never marry. Year after year he will refuse to go before the mayor or the priest.

This "celibacy of lovers" can also rise out of an authentic antisocial reaction. It may be a kind of refusal to enter into the system imposed by society. Beneath such an attitude there is always deep, unconscious, and intense fear of no longer being distinct and of having to do what everybody does, the fear of being caught in the network of adult relationships which go on for a time and end in death. Unquestionably, this grasp of the lifetime which leads to death is one of the major difficulties of the crisis of adolescence.

Frequently, celibacy of this kind is accompanied by some degree of alcoholism. Alcoholism is often a sign of anxiety or an unconscious fear of inferiority. The individual attempts to escape his fear in the atmosphere of a cafe, the exhilaration of semi-sobriety, and the illusory brilliance of a drink-freed tongue. The psychological situation conditioning alcoholism and negative celibacy may be exactly the same.

We should also point out that the female companion of such celibates is usually emotionally disturbed. Otherwise she would not get involved in such a situation or at least would break it off and leave her partner.

In classical literature Don Juan is married. We are right to suppose, however, that in today's world he would not be. In earlier times children were married by arrangements which could have no personal meaning for them. This is not the case today, and a twentieth-century Don Juan would not get married. The Don Juan type is one of the clearest cases of negative celibacy.

By the Don Juan type we mean the kind of man whose scandalous behavior Leporello sings about with his endless list of conquests: "In Spain . . . a thousand and three." Every woman, whatever her nationality, appearance, or even age, irresistibly excites him to seduce her in order that he might reject her immediately and go on to another. Beneath the theatrical exaggeration we find an easily observable type of man. Such behavior generally expresses a very neurotic psychosexual situation and is an indication of negative celibacy. In his own emotional development the Don Juan type is caught in a very disturbed attitude toward men and women. Generally he is afflicted by very intense and deep-seated, truly pathological anxieties. Suicide is not exceptional.

Every case, of course, has its own history and roots. Without going into great detail, we could not describe the typical psychogenesis of Don Juanism. All we will do is single out certain emotional attitudes which enter into such behavior.

Beyond doubt, the dominant attitude is a radical and agonizing uncertainty about his virility. The man is always pursuing his power to seduce in a quest which never satisfies him. Having seduced a woman proves nothing to him. Worse, it reawakens his unrest. He is seized by panic that he will not be able to seduce another. Above all, it revives his radical inability to maintain and consolidate the seduction he has barely initiated. For complex neurotic reasons he is profoundly incapable of responding honestly to the demand of a woman who reveals herself to him as a person. He flees and seeks madly to renew an experience which confronts and revives his anxiety but can never cure it.

As paradoxical as it may seem, the Don Juan type is impotent—not necessarily unable to experience coitus but impotent to establish a relationship of true, lasting, and deep love. As clinical observation demonstrates, more or less acute crises of physical impotence may also occur. The Don Juan type is a sick man who seeks continually to prove himself and never succeeds. His search is unconscious and always misses the mark. On the level of phantasms, that is, subconscious representations, the search may be after some mysterious object which doesn't exist.

Some authors stress the connection there can be between Don Juanism and unconscious homosexuality. Profoundly incapable of any intersubjective relationship, in the grip of an agonized narcissism, the Don Juan type is, along with his perpetual sexual obsession, somehow "dedicated" to celibacy.

There is another kind of celibate we might call the "retarded boy scout"—no discredit intended toward this admirable organization. At twenty he is all devotion to duty. He is doing well in his professional training. He keeps busy with his church youth group, trade union, athletic club, etc. He has apparently no sex life or love affairs. He goes steady now and again but it does not last. At thirty he is still all right. Progressing professionally and still dutiful and generous, warning signs of a turning into himself appear. A few confidants—a friend or spiritual director—who are aware of his personal life know that he masturbates bitterly and has passing affairs or goes occasionally to a prostitute. (I knew one who married and three days later his wife left him for good. Officially, he became once more what he had always been—a single man.) At forty-five he gradually becomes an "old bachelor": fussy, egocentric, peevish. By sixty he will be the old "character" who ogles shopgirls on the street.

What has happened to such a man? From the time of childhood, something blocks some boys' emotional development. Of course, cases differ greatly. Some boys never get through their adolescent crisis of sexual awakening. Fearful of the real commitment of sexual union, they take refuge in imaginary or sentimental eroticism and compensate themselves by some generous and often idealistic activity which hides their confusion.

They never escape the conflict over their aptitude for sexual relations. Often it brings on bitterness and churlish or finicky aggressiveness, a clear indication of a dramatic lack of fulfillment. The worst thing that can happen is that sometimes such men, because of family or social pressure, find themselves married without knowing why. Just as there are stable "celibate marriages," there are also "married bachelors." The word they pronounced before the marriage witnesses was not really their own. We wonder seriously what validity such marriages can have.

Differing in a few characteristics but very similar indeed is the celibate "Mama's boy." An inseparable widowed mother and her only son form a strange psychological "couple." We see women of seventy treating a son of forty-five as if he were only five years' old. And neither of them can escape. Such a man is incapable of hurting or contradicting his mother. He can leave her only for short periods and even then only with deep, complicated, and pointless unrest. Clearly there is no question of his marrying. That is for the best. If he did, he would impose his domineering mother on his wife, and that would turn out badly. Clinical experience furnishes us any number of examples.

He leads a tranquil, regular life. He seems happy and believes he is happy. Yet he seems easily upset. He has crises of violent anger which contrast with his habitual gentleness. He occasionally rebels against his mother but quickly stifles his rebellion in guilt feelings which torture him. When his mother dies, sometimes such a man marries, but the marriage rarely succeeds. He may remain a bachelor for the rest of his life.

In *Le Geranium Ovipare* Georges Fourest describes with bitterness and irony such a solitary man under the title "A Life." The poem ends: "and never having been very bold with women / he masturbated every Tuesday / after dousing the light. He died a virgin / having never suspected his concierge loved him."

The sexual and emotional life of such a celibate does not amount to much—masturbation and furtive recourse to a prostitute. Sometimes he becomes a regular client of the same girl. His relationship to women is such that he can scarcely do otherwise. The prostitute commits him to nothing and at the same time provides him more intense sensual emotion than do his solitary maneuvers. Unknown even to himself, there may also be a satisfaction in cheapening a woman in order to exorcise his mother's domineering image and avenge her hold on him.

What has happened to this man? His emotional development was blocked and distorted after he had already assumed his basic sexual direction, but it happened early enough to keep that direction from really affirming itself. His paralyzing relationship with his mother was established at five or six years of age. While his own sexuality is normal enough in its basic orientation, it remains at the stage of development it had reached at that early age. A schematic description like this is a little oversimplified but sums up the essentials of the situation.

According to modern psychology the example we have just seen introduces the complex problem of homosexuality. For many authors and clinical authorities influenced by psychoanalytic discoveries, masculine celibacy is often conditioned by latent homosexuality. We must explain this term carefully to avoid errors and confusion.

First a word of caution. As we attentively observe human beings and their problems, we quickly realize that this experience is literally *inexpressibly* complex in the concrete. Caught between the need to form clear ideas and our obligation to be faithful to experience, we tend to simplify and construct logical, if sketchy, definitions. The important thing is not to be misled by this procedure and not to reduce personal situations to these sketches. Personal life always infinitely transcends them. All they can do is introduce us to an understanding of reality.

Bearing in mind this indispensable precaution about our language, we can go on to say that the sexual instinct is manifested under two aspects. The more fundamental is the spontaneous emotional attitude toward others which is always based on sexuality. It is this emotional attitude which can develop into the *sentiment* of love and tenderness. The second aspect is the so-called erotic attitude. It is not really surprising that these two components of the sexual instinct can, during childhood and adolescent emotional development, become dissociated and develop progressively in distorted, contradictory, or unequal ways.

Homosexuality consists in the attraction which someone feels for persons of the same sex. Real life situations can be very diverse, however. This attraction may be sexual only in a generalized way. A man may enjoy himself more in the company of men—or of some particular man—than with women. This is what psychology means by latent homosexuality. It indicates an incompleteness of relational development and is marked by very variable and individual conditions.

This attraction may also be total—affectively and explicitly erotic: homosexuality as defined in common parlance. The attraction may never be expressed in outward behavior or, on the other hand, it may be displayed quite openly. It may be ambivalent—accompanied by a solidly affirmed heterosexual attraction. Every degree and every combination of tendencies is possible. Overt homosexuality is one of the most complex and central problems of clinical psychology. To complete our outline, a man's homosexual attitude may be exclusively erotic, while his generalized sexual relationships appear quite normal. We see men who are intensely in love with a woman, yet have no desire for her and carry on furtive, anonymous homosexual relations. The psychological situation between the man and the woman corresponds to platonic love.

Homosexuality, whether latent or overt, clearly implies celibacy, just as congenital blindness keeps people out of certain professions. Nonetheless, it is not rare to see explicit homosexuals marry, although almost always with tragic consequences. Latent homosexuality, as we have fitted it into our outline, conditions certain forms of negative celibacy which are otherwise inexplicable.

There are some men, for example, who are attracted to women—or to a particular woman—and enjoy seemingly normal heterosexual activity. They are, however, fundamentally incapable of achieving fulfillment by *living* in an intersubjective and stable relationship with a woman. We frequently see the case of a man who cannot enjoy the company of a woman. He is really happy only in the company of men—or a particular man—without necessarily feeling the slightest conscious homosexual desire. He may spend a few hours or a whole night with a woman but he is incapable of more than that. He is really ill at ease in the continual presence of women whom he cannot interiorly accept as persons. Irresistibly he feels at ease only in relations within his own sex. The climate in which he finds security has to be unisexual.

This psychological incapacity for stable heterosexual relationships can have extreme variations. It can be compatible with conjugal situations which are, on the whole, satisfactory to both parties. On the other hand, it may make married life practically unbearable. Robert Anderson's play *Tea and Sympathy* focused on this problem in the case of a professor whose wife leaves him for this reason. Incapacity of this kind can also make marriage completely out of the question.

A negligible degree of latent homosexuality is very frequent. The evidence of modern psychology dictates this conclusion which suggests so many questions. This evidence indicates that practically never does a person's sexuality *totally and definitively* coincide with his outward appearance to afford *absolute* emotional security. This is a fact that some have trouble accepting.

It is no surprise that we find this characteristic to an almost pathological degree among negative celibates. It is less important in the bachelor living in concubinage and more in the retarded adolescent or mama's boy. It is certainly a very important part of the make-up of the Don Juan type.

This homosexual element sometimes develops in the preconscious mind. During times of serious social disturbances, like the German Occupation of France from 1940 to 1945, men frequently discover themselves to be overt homosexuals—sometimes to their great surprise. The development failure which we term latent homosexuality has extremely varied causes which often operate on a very primitive level of emotional relationships. Psychoanalysis has revealed entirely new dimensions of understanding and therapy for this emotional problem which weighs so heavily on certain men.

The problem may be rooted in a maternal relationship. The child may not have been able to integrate the difference in sexual structure when he organized his earliest phantasms—psychic representations which precede the awakening of consciousness. He will always remain haunted by nostalgia for the sexual object—the phallus—that he primitively "lent" to his mother. Or, during his first years he may have been led to identify himself with a mother whose presence was predominant and unconsciously invasive and exclusive. Or, the child may have been negated in his own sexuality by a mother who would not admit that he was a man.

The interplay of such factors during an apparently normal development may cause an individual to be panicked by the crisis of adolescence and consciousness of normal sexual attraction. He may either remain immobile in this adolescent ambivalence or he may retreat to archaic manifestations of his sexuality. Fear of his father may forbid not only an official claim of virility, but virility itself.

These have been only a few simply stated examples of possible disturbances. Latent homosexuality—and overt homosexuality even more so—expresses a more or less primitive narcissism as well as a general emotional incapacity to relate to others. The problem centers primarily on relations with persons of the opposite sex. But relations with persons of the same sex will also be disturbed by projections, possessiveness, or reflex defensiveness. This should clarify what we earlier observed: negative celibates manifest their most important problems on the level of personal relationships rather than in their sexual activity as such.

This treatment has necessarily been superficial and rapid due to the nature of this book. In conclusion, we must say a word about negative celibacy conditioned by pathological and deeply ingrained perversions. Sadomasochism, fetishism, transvestism, bestiality, etc., do not necessarily prevent marriage. But the most negative and anguished celibacy is their usual expression.

NEGATIVE CELIBACY IN WOMEN

From the point of view of anatomy as it affects the first obscure outlines of a child's self-image, the only mark of distinction is sexual. A girl is the one "who does not possess. . . ." The absence of a tangible and accessible sexual organ and the "yawning abyss" which replaces it are discovered by a child very early. They are experienced as the "presence of a lack," as it were. Femininity is characterized as a question and an ambivalence. A girl's development revolves around this theme. She has to accept this lack which camouflages a concealed reality whose *immediate* discovery is impossible. In the process she will establish a firm and progressively more articulate bond with her father, "the one who does possess. . . ."

Negative celibacy in women expresses an emotional incompleteness just as it does in men. But there are some fundamental differences. Celibacy in a thirty-year-old woman does not pose as many social problems as masculine celibacy. At least in our civilization it attracts far less attention. This may indicate that the psychological problems of negative celibacy are less clear, more subtle, and less apparent than in men.

A primary feminine psychological problem which can condition negative celibacy concerns the demand for virility. The emotional climate in which the infant initiates and develops her personality may not allow her to accept in a positive manner her sexual nonphallic condition. Before any possibility of verbalization or even symbolic articulation, she will sense her sexuality—the culminating point of her self-apprehension—as an unjust punishment, a privation, an intolerable inferiority, none of which she can understand. Her reaction to this primitive, complex, and anguished experience which she cannot solve will condition her entire development. Without realizing it, she will have a profound tendency as a woman to establish relationships and behavior patterns in terms of this imaginary and primitive frustration.

The personalities of celibate women are very varied. There is, for example, the hyperfeminine and seductive woman who remains unmarried out of cruelty. She plays unconsciously with her femininity or rather with the effect it has on men. She accentuates it as if she were totally bent on seduction—a little like Don Juan. In actuality she cares only to seduce in order to vanquish, to put men at her mercy. Since her femininity signifies something completely negative, her ambition stops there.

She enjoys a superiority which offers her no advantage and has no meaning. She is, by definition, incapable of giving herself, which would represent precisely the expression of integrated femininity. The seduction ends in an impasse. Naturally, this makes the man rebel. The woman ends by using her anguish as a prop. This is the kind of woman we call a flirt. Her fate will vary according to the social milieu in which she finds herself. Her sentimental and sexual life has no importance. Such women are generally frigid as well.

Another case is the older girl who is a little mannish, a tomboy—common expressions which vividly express unanalyzed but profound intuitions. The girl is haunted by nostalgia for an impossible virility and tries to achieve it, instead of taking vengeance for not having it like the preceding type. Men do not interest such women since they themselves are unconsciously trying to act as if they were men.

They will remain—if we can risk this expression—actively celibate. They will become slave drivers, crusaders, suffragettes. They will tend to choose professions or activities usually reserved for men in their cultural milieu. If they are intellectually gifted and can develop their gifts, they will become professors, philosophers, but in a masculine style, as it were. This can even condition the ideological positions they may adopt more defensively than as a result of serene reflection. To give only one example, there are undoubtedly "contraceptive suffragettes" whose aggressive attitude is more motivated by sexual anxiety than by the real problems of birth control which scarcely concern them.

The sexual and sentimental life of these women is at least as limited as that of the previous type and they likewise are usually frigid. This kind of woman bothers men and strikes them as funny. It is as if men unconsciously felt more threatened by them than by the "flirts." But we must not forget that situations of this kind are conditioned by profound anxieties, often so much the more painful because they are obscure and contradictory. Added to this there is often the frustration of maternity both secretly desired and unthinkable.

Another case may involve a business woman who has no boyfriend. Under perpetual tension she lives in an insoluble contradiction. Elegant, refined, very feminine in appearance, she is authoritarian and harsh in her relationships. She constantly tends to "put people—especially men—in her pocket." She is frequently an efficient person and wears people out to get what she wants. They give in to her to keep peace. Her friends are in an uncomfortable position. They have little freedom to differ from her opinions. She despises women and enjoys humiliating men. Her amorous adventures are not rare but usually end in disaster. Their concealed basis is a terrible solitude.

All these women instinctively reject men which necessarily disturbs all their relationships. Just as with the men we discussed above, we wonder what part latent homosexuality plays in such women. The problem in women is much less simple than in men because femininity makes its first appearance as a "question about a lack." It seems that an emotional homosexuality is quite frequent but that directly genital manifestations of it are rare.

All clinical psychologists agree that the problem of feminine homosexuality is more confused and more difficult to observe than masculine homosexuality. The maternal need will play a role in the woman who has no man. A child or its symbolic equivalent can be an irrepressible necessity.

On the most obscure level of their unconscious, some such women desire a substitute sexual object to fill their void and reassure them in their fundamental insecurity. An infant is the ideal sexual object since it is their own. But this may be impossible or forbidden. In that case someone else's child or an equivalent symbolic animal may supply.

A cat, a dog, or goldfish often fill this compensatory role. Solitary women sometimes project their emotions onto their favorite animal with surprising intensity. Animals have the advantage of really compensating an insupportable loneliness. They also have the disadvantage that they die—which precipitates an emotional crisis. Just take a look at the inscriptions on tombstones in an animal cemetery. We are torn between laughter and indignation. In the last analysis, however, when a dog or cat dies, it can always be replaced.

Frequently, the symbolically substituted animal is not sufficient. In that case the solitary woman will desire—consciously or not—a child who comes from herself. I believe that the psychological rejection of men comes into play in one degree or another with a high proportion of unmarried mothers, most often without their realizing it. It is worth noting that the very expression "unmarried mother" underlines the contradiction in the underlying psychological attitudes.

A common clinical example can be given. A woman around forty, after a solitary and somewhat wild life, finds herself pregnant. The father wants to marry her, even insists on it. She refuses obstinately and breaks off the relationship. She is now going to live for her child. It is a boy. All seems well while the child is small but trouble begins when he reaches preadolescence. He knows absolutely nothing about his father of whom there is not a single trace, not even a photograph, in the home.

On his own he discovered that he must have a father since others have one. He has never been able to broach the problem with his mother who always avoids his questions. His adolescent crisis was dramatic—delinquency, running away from home, etc. Around twenty, the son manifests a radical ambivalence: he adores his mother and runs to her like a baby. At the same time he treats her with violent aggressiveness. As a young adult, he gradually develops into a situation of chronic illness. This allows him to be passively pampered and entertained by his wife (for he is *married!*), his aging mother, adults in general, even "mother social security." A complementary detail: there have always been in his mother's home two cats and three goldfish, real rivals of the son, especially when at six or seven he began to escape from his mother's apron strings. This need for a "child without a man" may be translated into the desire—and realization—of artificial insemination. Such things are not unheard of.

The very extremes of the example we have given are significant. They show clearly the profound emotional and sexual disturbances which can lie behind such cases and the distorted relationships, especially with the child, that may result. The number of disabled young men who have grown up in such a climate is literally overwhelming.

The other theme we can discern in certain feminine celibates is organized around what we can call "anxiety about incest." Some explanations are necessary. This expression could cause confusion because of the moral signification one might be tempted to give it. What we are talking about is an unconscious psychic process. It has no moral qualification. It takes place far beneath conscious apprehension and reflection on values.

In the course of her development, the girl-child may become fixed on the only one around her who is the possessor of what she does not have and who alone can give it to her—her father. It can happen that this normally transitory primitive stage may become blocked and the girl's deepest emotional attitudes may remain on this level. Certain unbalanced family situations, which may or may not be apparent, can provoke such an immobilization.

First as a girl, then in adolescence, she retains this unconscious desire for sex with her father. But this desire is forbidden in that particularly threatening way in which children view prohibitions. It becomes a direct source of fear and anxiety. Since the girl was immobilized on this level at a very primitive moment in her emotional development, she cannot distinguish men in general from her father. Every desire will awaken this old forbidden desire and the resultant anxiety. Even the most normal desire for men, born of full-blown sexuality, remains indissociably linked to this primitive and ambivalent desire, never resolved or surpassed, for her father who is the bearer of sex. Desire for a man and marriage are unconsciously forbidden. The attraction of love can never find any possible realization.

This leads us to the case of a young woman of thirty-five who has just consulted a physician for symptoms of nervous depression associated with an upsurge of religious sentiment. To the degree that she will talk about herself and evoke or state what has happened to her we notice that she has never fallen in love except with married men.

Perhaps there have been young men who loved her and spoke to her about marriage but none of them attracted her. If she has had an affair with any of the married men who do attract her, most of the time there is uneasiness, dissatisfaction, a kind of despair even, whose motivations are much more profound than any moral estimate of her behavior. The situation of such women can be truly tragic. Contrary to the woman without a man, they call for a man with all their being but this call is forbidden.

Similar problems condition the behavior of spinsters who "fall in love" with priests. A priest offers the advantage of being simultaneously free because he is celibate and sexually forbidden because he is consecrated. Even better, he is called "Father." This can be the ideal solution for a celibate woman in the situation we are projecting. She can fall madly in love with this "superman-father" with complete peace of mind since, at least in principle, she has nothing to fear from him sexually. Some of these women, when they speak to a priest or talk about him, have a way of saying "Father" that, without their realizing it, contains a veritable ocean of psychological voluptuousness. When two get attached to the same man, the most bitter and aggressive jealousies are likely to be unleashed.

Here again we must make an important distinction. Our first instinct is to mock and make fun of these "holy-water-fountain ladies." We must not forget that they live in emotional situations for which they are not responsible. Their behavior translates obscure disturbances, compensating as well as it can for an inner weakness and secret suffering which they are never able to express.

In an attempt to place different kinds of negative celibacy in a framework, we have projected only a few examples which have inevitably been limited to unsatisfactory and simplified outlines. These have been only high points which are indicative but cannot account for the diversity and complexity of real personal situations.

4. POSSIBLE VALUES OF NEGATIVE CELIBACY

It is a fact that there are many negative celibates in the world even though people seldom question themselves on the subject. The proportion who show serious signs of imbalance or breakdown is very small. These are the two poles of clinical observation. The immediate conclusion is that the state of negative celibacy, as neurotic and painful as it may be, is not incompatible with living a satisfactory life free from insurmountable crises or suicidal tendencies. A positive utilization of this negative situation is not only possible but extremely frequent.

A comparison can help us to reflect on this fact. A medical student decides early in his studies to specialize in surgery. He sets himself this goal which seems to him to offer the best chance of fulfillment. During the fourth year of his studies he contracts serious poliomyelitis which leaves him almost totally paralyzed in all his limbs. There is no longer any question of accomplishing the ambition which had been the center of his life.

He is going to have to ask himself some questions and think about activities which he never before had considered concrete possibilities. He will notice that embryology, for example, is a very exciting field and that he has never thought about it much. From now on, he decides, he will specialize in this field. His capabilities are made sharper by the necessity of living in the grip of a massive *paralysis*. He has a good chance of becoming a better embryologist than he would have been a surgeon.

We all know examples. The will-to-live-in-spite-of-all seems often to be multiplied tenfold by some problem which turns out in the end to be a paradoxical stimulant. As we have described it, negative celibacy is such a problem, a paralysis of the sexual instinct.

Clearly, this is only a comparison. At first sight the two "paralyses" have nothing in common. Nevertheless, the image is more valid than it may first seem. Poliomyelitis, of course, attacks a person physically but it profoundly affects as well the self-image that had been constructed and is now brought brutally into question in his own emotional self-evaluation. The paralysis which results from the psychosexual problems of negative celibacy is invisible and interior; but in a different fashion, it also affects the security of a person in his self-image and significance.

It is not surprising that this purely psychic paralysis can be—more often than might be thought—a real and paradoxical stimulant of the will-to-live-in-spite-of-all. This reflex defense, this will-to-live-in-spite-of-all reaction, instead of being conscious and reflective as in the case of polio, arises in toto out of the unconscious mind. Neurotics, in the broadest sense of the word, are made that way from earliest infancy, even if their symptoms do not reach consciousness or clinical observation until much later.

There is another frequently observed fact. Many individuals, even poorly endowed, sense certain problems, understand certain situations, refine their sensibilities or their capacity to operate in a certain area, thanks to their neurosis. To achieve this, there clearly must exist sufficient lucidity and some room to maneuver. In practice it happens much more frequently than a too systematic psychiatric viewpoint might lead us to believe. A doctor must never forget that in his office he sees only situations which require help. With a few mental gymnastics he could pick out all the other people in whom he can notice symptoms most people would never recognize. These people manage to disentangle their problems all by themselves and therefore can live with satisfactory autonomy.

When something is missing that ought to be present, it bothers us, and we think about it more than we would if it were present. We are much more occupied–sometimes preoccupied–with missing or aching teeth than with those with no problem. Let us press the paradox. We may realize that a certain food, which we never dreamed of eating before it was forced on us by circumstances, is actually excellent. We realize that we enjoy it and were wrong not to try it before. This is not at all to say that there is here a strict analogy with the emotional and purely psychic level of personality.

The obsessively scrupulous person will often be able to find for others the conforting words he needs himself but cannot manage to say to himself. A person who is not scrupulous might never find them at all. Often negative celibates understand the problems of marriage with infinite delicacy and are able to help married couples in their difficulties. They are tormented sufficiently by their own forced nonmarriage to be able to see into and sense problems which the married people themselves cannot see at all because they have no vantage point, they cannot get far enough away to view them in proportion. Let me hasten to add that this proposition needs to be relieved of certain false notes. Too many celibates tend to get mixed up in the marital problems of others and to project their own problems without realizing it—just as there are many maiden aunts whose desire for their nieces and nephews to marry is marked by fervor that is as touching as it is clumsy and sometimes destructive.[1]

Because of the very suffering it entails, the psychosexual paralysis of forced celibacy can open the person who undergoes it to perspectives of activity and fulfillment which he might never have discovered if he had been normal. It can have positive and valuable compensations. We can give only a few examples.

Unable to establish themselves sexually in their own eyes and in the eyes of others, some celibates instinctively establish themselves in an entirely different manifestation of themselves. They will be the ones to keep everybody laughing, the ones who are the life of the party and who give spirit to a reunion. They will be the amusing and original storytellers and the ones you can always ask for a favor. In short, these are the people you cannot do without.

[1] We would like to ask these good ladies a frightening question—which they would never understand: "Why do you *need* them to get married?"

Their friends may be somewhat surprised that they are not married. "Too bad. He (or she) is so nice." The idea seldom crops up, however. Even behind their back it is not discussed. He (or she) does not seem bothered by not being married, and so others are not either. If the question does come to mind, everyone says, "after all, it's none of my business." All of us, at some time in our life, have known this kind of single person. Maybe at home alone with himself he knows sad moments. But the remembrance of the evening he has spent has enough positive value to hang onto and, in spite of everything, he feels alive.

Another person will establish himself by intellectual success. As we said, the difficulties of psychosexual development are very precocious and take root well in advance of clear consciousness. We can accurately speak here of *sublimation.*

In an *unconscious* process the subject looks for and begins to find a valuable compensation for the forbidden or missing phallus. He will develop an organ of another kind but one which will be his own and will have value in the sight of others. Such sublimations are generally most successful in the area of the sciences. Confrontation with an external reality which imposes its own structure and question considerably limits flights into intellectual abstractions which easily become neurotically warped.

A negative celibate may also find satisfactory compensation and a consciousness of security about his place in society in professional success. We will discuss this possibility in terms of a sense of accomplishment.

Some brief explanation is necessary. Modern psychology indicates that one of the important moments in a child's emotional development arrives when he achieves mastery of his bowels. He realizes for the first time that he *does* something, that by his own energy he imposes a form on something that comes from himself, that something from his own substance separates from him so that he can *contemplate* and *offer* it. When these early experiences spark a spontaneous reaction by those around, they permit the child—in the course of progressively *sublimated* activities (in the technical sense, that is, prior to clear consciousness)—to construct a sense of security based on recognized accomplishment and a positive sense of existence.

This emotional stage, which the specialists call "anal," precedes the child's clear grasp of his sexuality. Only after he profoundly discerns his sex will the discovery of accomplishment exert its full force. An individual whose sexual development has been blocked or restrained can find satisfactory compensation in a sense of accomplishment, so long as nothing has seriously compromised his development in this direction.[2] Clinical observations demonstrate that this is frequently true. Negative celibates who find security in this sense of effectiveness in professional accomplishments are not rare. They bear their celibacy and make it bearable for others.

[2] Psychic personality is not cut in two: one part, sexuality; the other, aggressiveness. Both expressions of the ego are closely linked. Nevertheless, they can be distinguished and either one may grow to become predominant. Sexual problems will always color the aggressiveness but they may very well not *impede* its positive and consistent fulfillment.

There are even celibate professions, in which celibacy is logical, likely, and easily explainable, if not obligatory. A few examples: no one is surprised if a professor, a commando officer, or a social worker remains single. The Catholic ecclesiastical profession involves obligatory celibacy. We shall discuss this at length later.

For this kind of success to be sufficient for an individual and those close to him, his psychological state cannot be *overly* neurotic. Beyond question there are unconscious motivations for choosing certain professions. Everyone knows, for example, that the world of high fashion is full of homosexuals. Sometimes the choice of a teaching career is conditioned by latent homosexuality. Rarely, however, is this latter choice conditioned by an engrained habit of pederasty which leads to indiscreet behavior. When it does happen, a good deal of emotion results, but we must bear in mind that it is an exceptional case.

To end these reflections on the possible values of negative celibacy, we must briefly discuss the help provided by psychotherapy. Twenty years' experience demonstrates that psychotherapy can often facilitate the positive utilization of negative celibacy and can enable troubled individuals to better accept their situations. Complete honesty is certainly of the utmost importance for the positive utilization of any neurotic situation. An honest individual will be able to recognize and accept his problem even if he cannot elucidate all his profound conflicts. He will not be totally deceived by rationalizations even though he recognizes a strong tendency to let himself be deceived by them. He will be able to step away from himself and see possibilities in himself that would otherwise elude him.

A man may know, for example, that behind his passion for teaching or his love for children lies something not so simple and flattering. It may be a problem in relating to adults, or timidity, or emotional and sexual silence toward women. A woman may know that she is drawn to a career in social work not only by a desire for dedication and to lead others to a better life but to find some compensation for obscure personal dissatisfaction. The idea of marriage may never have seemed desirable. The man may know that he is a homosexual. He may have realized it even as late as twenty- or twenty-five-years-old. He suffers because of it but he does not hide what it means from himself.

Individuals like these can work out their compensations with a healthy cynicism, a sense of humor we might say, which does not let them be hoaxed by the illusion of being a pure spirit. This lucidity is certainly the key to the discovery of the positive values of negative celibacy and whatever conditions it. Psychotherapy can often help someone achieve this kind of lucidity.

I must define what I mean. By psychotherapy I mean any relationship designed to help an individual with psychological or psychosomatic problems. The therapeutic agent is exclusively the relationship itself and the exchanges that express it rather than a physical or chemical medication. Such a relationship is extremely delicate. The therapist, whether he knows it or not, is the direct therapeutic agent—both doctor and medicine. Modern psychology shows how important and intense the emotional implications of such a relationship are—on the unconscious or pre-conscious level—for *both* parties. This is the central problem, which is technically called transfer and counter-transfer, of any therapeutic relationship. Any psychotherapy which gets underway without the therapist recognizing this central problem—which concerns him as much as the other person—runs the risk of catastrophe. It will at best make the problem more acute. An example will help.

X, thirty-years-old, has just found a psychologist, who may or may not be a doctor, or a spiritual director. The person in question is either ignorant of the insights of psychoanalysis or refuses to accept them. Or, still worse, he accepts psychoanalytic theories intellectually but not as something which concerns him personally. X tells him that he is full of torment. He would like to marry and have children but there is no question of doing so because he is homosexual and feels no attraction for women. The psychologist questions him—but he fails to ask himself if these questions are motivated by his own unconscious desires, for example, a desire to act superior. He offers a few generalities on the Oedipus complex. Then he tells X: "It's all in your mind. Let your natural instincts go. Have a few drinks and find a prostitute and let yourself go."

The result is simple. Either X will not go to a prostitute because of pretended concern for moral principle, which does not impede the homosexual affairs he deplores, or he will go and the experience will be so completely disappointing that he will be more trapped than ever in his homosexuality. The so-called psychologist has understood nothing of X's problem. He has instead offered without hesitation his own reaction to homosexuality. Not for one instant did he ask himself if he really wanted X to achieve successful sexual relations or not, and why.

Nothing is more difficult or more dangerous than giving advice or direction. "Do this or do that . . ." What does it mean for the therapist as well as for the patient? Only psychotherapy based on psychoanalysis is capable of offering any real help. Real psychoanalysis is a lengthy and burdensome undertaking, even leaving aside the question of cost. For complex interior reasons or simply because of circumstances, many individuals simply cannot envisage it as a possibility. Many people, however, can be helped very effectively, sometimes even spectacularly, by a much shorter psychotherapy which does not attempt a radical solution but allows them to understand and find themselves and so be able to live autonomously. After all, this too can be very valuable.

This kind of psychotherapy, which steers clear of too overwhelming discoveries and at the same time respects the autonomy of the patient, is perhaps more delicate and difficult to handle than authentic psychoanalysis. It demands an experienced therapist who is even more alert and has thoroughly studied and experienced the workings of analysis.

Many individuals with problems—and particularly the negative celibates we are discussing—would definitely benefit from this kind of brief and superficial psychotherapy. Such a course demands that the therapist be particularly prudent, humble, and experienced in the workings of the unconscious mind. I have no hestitation in saying that it is better to have no treatment than to have psychoanalysis that is blind, moralistic, or just friendly but constantly risks dangers that the psychologist never even suspects.

5. FURTHER REFLECTIONS

If we can believe the statistics, there are more women than men in Europe and North America due to a higher proportion of female births, the premature death of men, and several other factors. It is mathematically logical, then, that a certain number of women will remain single because there simply are no husbands available. There is no point in stressing that such reasoning is completely theoretical. Nevertheless, the question remains: are there individuals who remain single without any subjective reason, that is, neither by choice nor because psychologically they are negative celibates, conscious or not? It is possible, at least in theory, because it is impossible to know what takes place in every individual case.

In our civilization the man generally takes the initiative in seeking marriage. As a result, we might tend to think—perhaps too simplistically again—that if a man does not take the initiative and remains single without any apparent motive, he has a problem. On the other hand, a young woman may never be asked and may remain single against her disposition and desire. This also is possible. But we have all noticed that there are girls who would seem difficult to provide for and yet get married, sometimes quite young, while there are others who have everything a man could want, and no one ever dreams of asking them.

Again there is the question why certain girls never stir up a proposal. It certainly cannot be explained by lack of money or charm or even by physical homeliness. In the light of modern knowledge about emotional psychology, I immediately tend to think that some secret, perhaps well-compensated, motive related to negative celibacy is at work. When such is the case, the woman's suffering can be intense. Since the cause is not neurotic tension, however, the problem is more easily surmounted and she runs less risk of serious and lengthy disturbance.

The existence of families of celibates helps us ascertain, if not understand completely, the psychological character of negative celibacy and its origin in the experienced relationships of infants. There are families of five or six children in which only one gets married. The others become spinsters and bachelors in a kind of implicit solidarity which manages to coexist with perpetually refueled and obvious conflicts.

When we examine such situations, we generally discover that the sexual relationship of the parents, in spite of an appearance of stability, was very neurotic. The sexual taboos and anxieties which we find in the children of such couples make us wonder how and under what conditions they could have produced children at all. It reminds me of the humorous passage in Daninos: the mother of Major Thompson's first wife advises her daughter before marriage that when "the moment" arrives, she should close her eyes and think about England.

A psychologist cannot help asking himself questions

when he sees families in which five out of six children enter religious orders. Clinical practice finds a fair number of sometimes serious neurotic troubles or delayed crises in such cases. This is an observable fact and it would be dishonest not to mention it.

When we discussed negative celibacy in women and the sexual object some women use to compensate themselves, we mentioned in passing that this object could be someone else's child. We must return to that because it brings up the problem of a single woman adopting an infant. Superficially, the adoption of one or more children would seem the ideal solution for a single woman. It would relieve her solitude, and her devotion would afford the abandoned children the benefit of affection they would otherwise miss. Such reasoning, however, totally misconceives the real and extremely delicate problem of adoption as clarified by modern psychological research.

All truly human education ought to help a child to become an adult of his own sex—conscious, autonomous, and well-balanced. We must carefully weigh everything in the climate of the child's life, that is, in his human environment, to see if it is likely to help or hinder his development. The first thing to be desired is that this climate be able to weather the successive awakenings of his self-consciousness. These only occur, as psychoanalysis shows, within and through the relationships he experiences with the *sexed* human beings around him. From this point of view, the adoption and education of a child by a celibate woman poses some great problems.

The first difficulty arises because the child is placed in a climate in which there is no man. His absence is not only material, or geographical, but psychological as well. Unconsciously or not, the negative celibate woman lives in a kind of rejection or neutralization of men as such, that is, in a neutralization of her own sexuality. In a certain sense, the climate in which the child will have to find *his own sexuality* implicitly negates sexuality. The child is going to have grave problems in finding himself, especially in terms of the primordial question of sexual duality which will dawn on him in the Oedipal crisis. Normally this would be solved by identification with the parent of the same sex. A boy will have trouble in taking himself for a man if he lacks any reference to an adult man recognized as such by his mother. A girl risks identifying herself with this mother precisely insofar as she rejects men.

Another difficulty can complicate or, oddly enough, sometimes correct the first one. The mother and child establish a relationship which is systematically reduced to a single dimension–dual but without reference to another. On the mother's side the danger is that the relationship will be unconsciously *possessive* and the child will become an object rather than a subject. The negative celibate woman is not protected from this instinctive possessiveness by her relationship to a husband.

Moreover, as soon as the compensatory object, the adopted child, is present, the psychological impossibility of a heterosexual relationship accents and consolidates her tendency to possessiveness. Later on, this will provoke the young adult to spectacular revolts. These rebellions are usually reflex defenses and quite healthy but they are rarely well-adjusted and constructive. People will talk about ingratitude without understanding the real meaning of the crisis. If the mother is a strong personality and the child is constitutionally less dynamic, such a situation can lean to premature paralysis of the child's development and sometimes to psychotic results. Without understanding what has actually happened, people will tend to blame the unknown heredity of the child who was adopted at a month old "without our knowing anything about his background."

The adoption of a child by a couple who are childless for medical reasons can pose problems which we should recognize: compensation, bitterness, unconscious aggressiveness between the man and woman because of their sterility, possibly unconscious aggressiveness toward the child whose presence continually reminds the couple of their problem. But if there is a good relationship between the adoptive parents, these problems can be resolved, granted a minimum of information and lucidity. It is not the same with the adoption of a child by a celibate woman. The very principle of such an adoption is open to question.

Masturbation is a common, transitory, and not alarming sign of the crisis of psychosexual awakening in adolescence. This is an established fact which is no longer under serious discussion. It may pose some problems for moral theory and for the personal moral development of the individual concerned. But of itself it absolutely does not hold the threat of disaster brandished by sixteenth-and-seventeenth-century morality and medicine. Here and there traces of these irrational fears still linger. Within the general context of the psychology of some individuals, masturbation may sometimes indicate the first manifestation of neurosis. Usually, however, it signifies only a difficult moment in fitting sexuality into the developing adult personality.

When everything goes normally, this autoerotic phase tends to resolve itself spontaneously. Generally, to the degree that an individual achieves the psychological aptitude for a stable sexual relationship, that is, for marriage, masturbation or its equivalents will disappear. To the degree that a human being is capable of loving another under the eyes of the third-party witness, he becomes capable of sexual continence, without even thinking much about it.

Negative celibacy always expresses an incompleteness or blocking of personal psychosexual development, whatever the dimensions of the problem may be. It is no surprise that this kind of celibacy is often accompanied by sexual difficulties—often uncontrollable manifestations of a badly adjusted, more or less repressed, sexual instinct. This instinct remains deeply mired in neurosis or in an adolescent crisis that has never been resolved. The solitary search for orgasm becomes an automatic release for emotional tension which is more confused than directly erotic. It develops as the result of conflicts which escape clear consciousness. When emotional tension develops on a conscious level, an individual can deal with it directly and autoerotic desire will not be aroused.

Recourse to prostitutes represents a habit closely linked

to the tension of masturbation: fear of women, reduction of women to objects, incapacity for intersubjective relationships. It may represent a timid attempt to pass from pure imagination to the "real thing." But it may also express a very disturbed (sometimes literally perverted–in the medico-psychological, not the moral, sense) relationship toward women. According to whatever testimony is available from the women involved, it is not exaggerated to say that among adult clients of prostitutes there is a high proportion of more or less emotionally disturbed cases.

The sexual difficulties prevalent among negative celibates of both sexes often complicate their problem. They are hard, sometimes even impossible, to overcome. Often they cause real anxiety which may not be immediately apparent. These orgasms, however they come about, amount to nothing; they "open into a void." They brutally force the individual to confront his own incapacity for mature intersubjective sexual relationships. Without his realization and against his will, they feed his problem and cause it to reoccur.

They have often lived in a very complicated atmosphere troubled by emotional guilt. The profound sexual conflicts which condition these problems almost always involve primitive fear and anxieties which become conscious as a sense of being guilty without knowing why. These developments only cause the primitive anxiety to revive and grow stronger. When moral education has placed an excessive accent on sexual problems–an all too frequent case–individuals may be caught in a vicious circle; their guilt leads to masturbation which in its turn revives the guilt. We can only help such individuals to improve their sexual balance by leading them to clearly distinguish between the moral aspects of the problem and these agonizing emotional releases which are of an absolutely different nature.

To close these remarks, it may be useful to point out another frequently observed problem. I refer to the kind of celibacy which is apparently imposed by some visible circumstance independent of the individual's will. The clearest example is some evident physical infirmity caused by sickness or accident: paralysis, mutilation of the limbs or the face, etc. To understand such cases, we must see that they often are not as simple as they appear.

A wounded veteran with both legs amputated or a quadriplegic polio victim may marry and experience a sexual relationship which may be difficult but is positive and successful. Someone else with a hand amputated or an arm paralysed will remain celibate because of his infirmity. In the latter case we are probably dealing with something else. Attentive clinical observation shows that for certain individuals who are already virtual celibates, a relatively unimportant physical disability may be the convenient pretext to legitimize a problematic emotional situation in the eyes of others. Evidently this reflex attitude is totally unconscious. Certain individuals bear their physical handicap with a serenity and courage which are really relief at having a plausible reason to explain their celibacy. This does not rule out quite admirable courage on a much more conscious level.

It is clear that the best way to help such individuals—

or at least not to complicate their problem—is to "play their game," to respect their alibi, and not to try to convince them that they should marry despite their problem. The only reason for trying to so convince them would be to exorcise their unrest and subjective and obscure anxiety which have nothing to do with their physical condition.

III

CLINICAL STUDY OF POSITIVE CELIBACY

6. POSITIVE CELIBACY

KEEPING TO OUR ORIGINAL DEFINITIONS, celibacy indicates the status of one who does not express, in the hearing of a witness who represents social authority, the word which would commit him to a stable sexual union. Up to now, we have discussed individuals impeded from pronouncing this word of commitment to sexual union by various *unconscious* and usually completely misunderstood conflicts. We called this "negative celibacy." We saw also that an existential commitment of this kind expressed in sexual activity is not indispensable either to the life or to the fulfillment of any individual. The sexual drive in its general sense is certainly fundamental and powerful. At the same time, it represents a tendency toward an activity which is optional and, in a certain sense, *secondary* to the formation and growth of the individual.

There seems to be room for a kind of celibacy which is not negative but instead expresses the need to find fulfillment and self-realization beyond or aside from that represented by socially adjusted sexual union. By definition such individuals would have to possess real psychological capacity for such a personal sexual commitment. We know clinically that there are such individuals. We shall call their situation "positive celibacy." It is more common than one would think. Their friends know them to be celibate but they are not so labelled and their celibacy poses no problems. *As celibates* they go unnoticed.

We speak of positive celibacy in the singular because we are not dealing now with "cases," individuals with more or less serious neurotic problems. We are concerned with an attitude which transcends the categories of strict science and is of an entirely different order. It is not a proper subject for clinical observation. We speak of digestive problems in the plural but of normal digestion in the singular. If someone who has no digestive problems wishes to go on a diet, that is his business, not the doctor's. The comparison is inadequate though, because nourishment is indispensable for life, while sexual activity is not. However, even its very inadequacy may make the tenor of our discussion clearer.

Without getting lost in a purely fictitious and imaginary ideal, we can suggest the personality traits of the typical positive celibate, male or female. I think that, if we reflect on it, we have all met persons of this type. Suddenly we say to ourselves, "Hey! That's right. He's single." Their personalities, of course, differ greatly; indeed, they are often quite singular. Yet, they are quite agreeable and do not strike us as eccentric. Naturally, there will always be weaknesses of character, reactions which are not perfectly adjusted, moments which are less serene. Ideal human balance–in marriage as well as in celibacy–is never fully and definitively achieved once and for all.

The first characteristic we discover is that the positive celibate is spontaneously at ease in the situations he faces.

He does not appear disconcerted when he encounters any particular kind of personality. He is not naturally belligerent, bitter, or bad-tempered. Bothersome people tend rather to amuse him, as if they did not directly concern him. Even though he is always considerate of others, he remains very independent, very superior, and very autonomous. He accepts life—the continual and varied encounters with his equals—with a philosophy that is both very alert and serene.

For example, if he must deal professionally with a superior who is anxious to be catered to, he calmly accepts him as he is. Without a second thought he can take such a man's personality into account and see to it that everything goes smoothly, without losing his self-possession or the sense of his own dignity. It does not even disturb him to have this superior contradict him, although he may be as certain as possible that he is in the right.

He accepts it as perfectly normal that a female coworker who does not see eye-to-eye with him would call his attention to some detail he had not noticed. Such cooperation seems natural to him and leads him to an understanding he would never achieve by himself. If he must deal professionally or socially with a single woman who is seductive, aggressive, or domineering, he quite simply avoids being victimised. As we emphasized about emotional maturity in general, this type of individual has developed satisfactory sexually based emotional attitudes.

This type possesses a flexible personality and the capacity to grow. It was Anatole France who said, "Only imbeciles do not grow." Intelligence, however, is not the point. The imbecility that hinders growth—the ability to adapt to ever-changing reality—is an *emotional* weakness. Some very gifted intellectuals are terribly stagnant. Other much more ordinary people manage to be always realistic and to modify their points of view. Whether the positive celibate is intellectually gifted or not, he gives two main impressions: sureness of his convictions on any subject and at the same time consciousness that all his opinions are relative. He is ready to review his position whenever necessary. He is capable of admitting to himself and to others, if need be, that he has not seen the entire picture, that he was mistaken or that he needs to reflect on some new fact. In other words, he has the ability to face any fresh question that the world poses to him.

He is "young," whatever age he may be. He refuses to become trapped in any philosophical, political, or relational system as if it were an immutable framework which he needs to balance his own fears. This is a remarkable personality trait in anyone, married or celibate. Even when such persons are quite old, we say, "It is astonishing how young he or she is!" In the case of the unmarried, in my opinion, this is a clear indication of positive celibacy. There is a sharp contrast when they are compared to "old fogies" or "old maids."

Another trait of positive celibacy is a very real and discreet respect for others as persons, exhibited in all sorts of relationships. While this characteristic involves keeping others at a respectful distance, it is not at all the same as aloofness or indifference. Indeed, it is just the opposite. The positive celibate is so completely at ease with himself that he puts even an importunate questioner at ease by a kind of objective welcome special to himself. It is not that he does not care about the other person; he is able to listen without exhibiting his judgment of him.

Celibates are frequently taken as confidants and counselors. One can tell them everything. They help us to see things clearly without imposing their own point of view. Maybe they will not be able to give clear and decisive advice, but after a talk with them one will realize better what to do. This characteristic is a very clear criterion of positive celibacy. Negatively celibate persons tend to butt into what is none of their business.

Positive celibates are generally very active and have many contacts and numerous and varied relationships. They are very involved in various aspects of social life and their activity is balanced and efficient. Because they are single their activity can be more extensive and time-consuming than that of the married people who are associated with them. They will realize that a colleague cannot take on more than a certain amount of union activity, for example, without neglecting his family. They will volunteer: "I'll take care of that; I'm free; if you do it, your wife and kids will never see you." If we get at all involved beyond the limit of our own immediate preoccupations, we quickly realize that men and women of this type are extremely helpful and that one is fortunate to find them. Indeed, it is almost essential that there be people like this.

These particular single persons are manifestly happy to spend themselves. At the same time, we realize that we must not abuse them; they will not allow themselves to be walked on. Their availability is clearly greater than that of married people but it is not unlimited. They possess a perfectly consistent life of their own which they protect quite tranquilly. They are quite capable of saying "no" when this life would be encroached on; but even this they can do without causing recriminations or resentment. They need moments of solitude: to read, to relax, to cultivate their interests. They need time to be with a few intimate friends; they are often very close to one or two families. They lead a very balanced life which does not manifest any hidden fundamental suffering.

Such celibates are neither prudish nor bawdy. They are not shocked by Rabelaisian remarks and can take active part in such conversation. They would not dream of refusing an invitation to a more or less risqué Go-Go Club. On the other hand, their interests are varied and such an idea does not occur to them automatically because of some inner need. It would never occur to them to slip discreetly into a burlesque show once or twice a week. In other words, their sexuality—in the more precise sense of the sexual instinct—is not a bother or burden to them.

What determines the emotional attitude that underlies the kinds of behavior we have been describing? These individuals enjoy a well-established basic emotional security. They are "sure of themselves," but not in the pejorative sense that this expression can suggest. Rather they are sure of who they are and are satisfied to be themselves. This attitude is built on a calm and honest appraisal of both their potentialities and their limitations.

This implies a good sense of humor, a real sense of detachment in looking at oneself—taking oneself realistically but not too seriously or tragically.

This basic security is clearly not the exclusive property of a few celibates. Many married persons also evidence it. It is the primary element in the success of marriage as well as in positive celibacy. This is worth pointing out in passing. Psychologically speaking, such security indicates mature emotional development which was not seriously blocked within the family by profound disturbances or major infantile fears. From birth such individuals were able to establish a satisfactory pattern of their own identity because they received natural and open love. To give one example, their parents did not feel deceived and disappointed because their child was a boy when they absolutely wanted a girl. These individuals were able to achieve their first experience of autonomous activity—anal experience—without any ambiguity. This inaugurated a progressive sense of being recognized in their early attempts at activity.

They were also able to accept their sexual anatomy without anxiety or unresolved fears. During the very complex confrontation with parents which precedes a child's temporary stabilization during the period of latency (from six or seven years' old to puberty), they were able to integrate their sex into the personal self-consciousness built on their earliest unconscious impressions.

They were able to grow steadily—to take their own measure as human beings—by gradually renouncing the initially necessary image of their parents as almighty and infallible. In coming to realize without panic the *relativity* of their parents, they were able to begin to accept a *relative* estimation of themselves. They therefore felt no anxiety over being merely themselves. The elements of self-esteem, fundamentally necessary in order to love others, were firmly established. Their adolescent crisis passed with a minimum of normal disturbances and inevitable conflicts. Very soon they gave evidence of the kind of self-reliance which is the very opposite of having to prove one's independence. In short, these are men and women who are almost completely adult (no one is ever totally adult). But why do such individuals remain celibate? As we observe their lives, we are tempted to tell ourselves that they would have made excellent spouses and fine parents. Almost irresistibly we add "it's too bad" without specifying "too bad" for *whom.* Probably not for them, since they do not seem to suffer on account of their state; indeed, they seem to have *preferred* it but not because they rejected or failed to recognize the value of marriage.

Their state of life expresses a preference. Whatever the personal motives for this preference may be—we shall examine this question later—it demonstrates something which may seem strange: a human being can view some other form of self-realization as preferable to sexual union. He may prefer a kind of personal commitment which is not compatible with married life. Since these persons believe sexual experience achieves full value only within marriage, they are generally spontaneously continent.

The implication is that human love, which naturally presents itself as ideal fulfillment, is actually not the last word in such fulfillment. Certain individuals see this quite clearly. In the final analysis, a human love which would absorb them does not seem *absolutely* satisfying. Though they accept such love as having a primary value, in the end it nevertheless seems an insufficient response to their personal aspirations.

But these positive celibates perceive the fundamental dialectic and ambivalence of sexual love in an entirely different manner from negative celibates. The latter feel this ambivalence as a profound uneasiness which at best they can compensate. It renders them incapable of achieving positive and stable human love. This is the source of their suffering—whether or not they admit it and whether or not they understand its meaning. Against their will they are somehow excluded from the possibility of satisfactory human love. They experience its relativity in terms of their own inner contradictions. Being alive they feel its attraction but they are never able to give themselves to it.

The positive celibate perceives this same relativity within the context of the relativity of everything temporal. This causes a more subtle and deeper suffering which is paradoxically less acute and more bearable because he can tell himself that his dilemma is, after all, *the* central question of conscious life.

It is likewise impossible for marriage, the positive and socially organized fulfillment of sexuality, to sidestep time —or death. Marriage has a history which unfolds in a succession of moments. One realizes that it will end in a cessation, a rupture of living experience, even if this certitude is rejected or placed within parentheses. This certainty directly contradicts the individual's awareness of himself as *existing*.

Love, the inexpressible and conscious bond between persons, is necessarily experienced as independent of duration, succession, cessation. We experience love not only as something which ought to last indefinitely but also as the only element of our existence which is of another order than the temporal. Precisely to the degree that married life is a mutually conscious dialogue, the partners grasp this insoluble contradiction. They achieve this through and in each other and in the very experience of the ambivalency of their success in love.

Others perceive this contradiction before they have involved themselves in marriage. From then on they dedicate themselves to whatever can broaden their satisfactory relationships and raise them outside of time. They feel that they can affirm themselves outside the temporal as far as possible by noninvolvement in the rich but markedly temporary experience of marriage. This clearly demands the cohesive emotional solidity which is the most profound element of that basic security which we have discussed. They are so sure of existing that consciously or not they seek to surpass time and sidestep death.

7. MEANINGFUL MOTIVATIONS

OUR CONSCIOUS MOTIVATIONS elude classification and specific description. Each person's emotional and spiritual life is unique. We can only propose a few examples and suggest superficially the inexpressible development of a real personality.

Among the first examples to come to mind is the survivor of a love which premature death has kept from being fulfilled in marriage. The survivor never marries. Without even reflecting on it and without forming any special attitude, he remains faithful to a love fulfilled through and beyond death itself. When we observe such cases, we are struck by their fundamental serenity, even when they lack any explicit religious reference. Such a form of celibacy seems to occur more frequently among women, although male examples may be observed.

In any case, this example seems very significant because it is based on a concrete relationship with another person. This relationship endures and passes to a level where it literally transcends sexual expression even though it remains essentially sexual. We are involved with the most complex question: a certain kind of absence or, more exactly, distance constitutes the most real kind of presence.

Everyday experience can approximate the idea. The Smiths understand and love each other very deeply. Of course, there are the normal disagreements, attacks of bad humor, household quarrels, but these do not affect the essentials of their relationship. By force of some extrinsic circumstance, one of them must be away on a trip for several months. Without thinking about it each will experience the other, somehow refined of the little idiosyncracies which cause annoyance in daily living but which now seem negligible and hitherto ridiculously exaggerated. The other person appears in his essential reality, in his true make-up, in his own person properly speaking. No longer is their tenderness constrained or blocked by the petty disagreements which each realizes afterward is as much his fault as the other's.

In a word, their love grows deeper. Indeed, this absence can sometimes be a test of it. Such a relationship occurs necessarily in a context which is not specifically sexual. In such circumstances a normal married man will desire his wife and be disturbed that she is away. But he would not be moved to masturbation by his thoughts about her. It scarcely occurs to him to think of other women. The geographic separation which seems at first sight to be absence is actually a particularly intense kind of mutual presence somehow removed from sexual temporality.

Frequently, widowhood which follows a long and successful married life produces this new kind of presence which expresses itself beyond sexual temporality. The words and attitudes of persons in such situations may sometimes seem childish and sentimental but they actually represent a very profound maturity.

In a celibate the same phenomenon produces what we might call "widowhood outside the fact." The beloved, whose death inaugurated this absence which is really a new kind of presence, seems more definitively alive and present in the survivor's experience than ever. In the same way, one may learn that a woman no longer young is "Miss." "I would have thought she was a widow," we say. And still no one realizes that she has loved and loves still —independently of sexual temporality.

From an entirely different point of view, we also observe individuals for whom relationships of lesser intensity but greater extension have more meaning than the commitment of marriage. They find very positive and indeed greater satisfaction in some form of philanthropic activity—in the most serious and realistic sense of the word—than in marriage. Marriage attracts them but it would contradict or be incompatible with this greater attraction. Beyond doubt, celibacy accepted for the sake of "dedication" is very ambiguous. A psychologist will always be on his guard, suspecting an alibi which justifies or camouflages a more or less neurotic negative celibacy.

But it is quite certain that this motivation can also authentically express a profound consciousness of the human drama and human solidarity. The need to participate in humanity's struggle may be perceived quite clearly and felt overwhelmingly. Besides, such a celibate can be distinguished as positive very quickly because he will act according to the characteristics we discussed earlier. He will be effective rather than a hindrance.

The most common motivation for celibacy is certainly

religiously oriented. We are here talking about *positive* celibacy—without meaning to imply in any way that there are not religious motivations for celibacy which are alibis for neuroses. On the contrary, alibis of this kind are very common because they offer the most effective justification. We shall leave aside examples of negative celibacy based on a religious alibi. That would lead us back to our earlier discussion.

The rejection or bypassing of the so-called carnal aspect of sexuality is found in a number of religions. Among others, we can mention the Roman Vestals whose vow was temporary, different Hindu sects, Buddhist bonzes in general, whose celibacy is also usually temporary, certain religio-philosophical sects of ancient Greece, and the Palestinian Essenes contemporary with Christ.

Sexuality and religion have always had a problem. There is a tendency either to adore sex in its loftiest significance as the source of life—for example, phallic worship in Hinduism—or to consider it the manifestation of the "evil deity" as in Manichean dualism.[1] Indeed, whether one is a believer or not, the Christian conception of sex seems the only one able to dissipate and clarify this age-old tension and give a clearly positive meaning to religiously motivated celibacy.

This view, elaborated in the complete panorama of Biblical revelation, places sexuality at the very heart of the world as God created it to be. In Genesis the naturally

[1] Pastor Max Thurian, in *Marriage and Celibacy* (Allenson: 1959), points out to what degree a Christian author like Tertullian was influenced by a latent Manicheism, for which sex, falsely identified with "the flesh," was in itself evil.

sacred character of sexuality in marriage is forcefully accented: "God saw that it was good. . . ," "Increase and multiply. . . ," "They will be two in one single flesh." Christ takes up the same theme and adds that "man must not separate what God has united." This is a clear affirmation that sexual differentiation somehow enters into the human creature's likeness to the Creator. This differentiation implies both the *duality* of persons and the fundamental drive to *unity within distinction*—the elementary dynamism of love.

God reveals himself as *being* love; and he reveals himself as infinitely beyond sex. His distinctive unity is trinitarian while sexuality, as we said in the first section, never transcends duality. Nevertheless, in Sacred Scripture the symbolic significance of married love has a privileged place: through it God progressively reveals the evolving relationship between himself and the human race.

The history of human love and sexuality is dramatic, as Father Grelot points out in *The Human Couple in Scripture*. "Something" introduces an insoluble contradiction into the very heart of the human condition. This is a mystery strictly so-called: an evident reality in which we are totally involved but which eludes our complete comprehension and our solutions. "Original sin" is the traditional description of this mystery which transcends language. By a kind of "turning in on itself" which prevents it from hearing God's word of love, the human race has become the prisoner of time, duration, and death—which contradict his word. It has become the prisoner of duality and time.

In the development of revelation, it gradually becomes

clear that God's plan of salvation is to be completed by the resurrection. Christ explicitly defines this context as the goal of everything—its ultimate meaning and climax —by his abiding presence and its sign: "He who eats my flesh and drinks my blood has life in him and I shall raise him up on the last day." It is no longer just a vague and more or less mythological speculation such as the Greeks were willing to discuss: Paul's ironic reception at the Areopagus gives an example of that. Nor does it any longer concern an obscure abode of the dead like the Sheol of the Old Testament.

This is the explicit announcement of a completely fulfilled "world" whose coming all nature, expressing itself through us, awaits "in travail," as St. Paul says. A new world will exist in which everyone will be definitively conscious of himself in the completely renewed totality of his psychosomatic personality and in the fulness of love. Its conception is realistic, even while it simultaneously remains totally unimaginable.

St. Paul's phrase about the "pangs of childbirth" suggests a comparison which is quite acceptable to modern psychology: in our personal destinies death appears as the second and definitive stage of birth. Each of us develops within the maternal uterus; then we emerge into time with its ambivalence, where we receive our first knowledge of intersubjective relationships; finally we achieve definitive development through the "birth of death."

We are presently in the same position relative to death and what it will reveal as we were in our mother's womb relative to our birth. A week before birth we were incapable of forming a single "idea" about the looks or personality of our father, who had after all placed us there. Nevertheless, even at that stage we were ourselves and not somebody else.

The idea of a personal resurrection had not acquired currency with all sectors of Jewish thought at the time of Christ. On the occasion of a controversy with the Sadducees about this subject Christ clarified the ultimate significance of sexuality. The Sadducees—the integralists of their time—did not accept the resurrection of the dead because it was not literally contained in the primitive texts attributed to Moses. They formed, so to speak, a reactionary party. To confound Christ on the resurrection, they submitted the case of a woman who had successively married six husbands, each of whom had died before producing a child: "Whose wife will she be in the world of the resurrection?"

Christ's answer (Luke, 20:34 ff.) is very clear. The world of the resurrection is no longer sexual: "they who are called to it" (the whole human race, as we know) are not married—they are no longer "under the dominion of death." The relationship between sexual activity and time is explicit. It is striking to compare this with what modern biological and psychological reflection has to say.

The world of the resurrection is sexed but no longer sexual. Sexual *activity*, having fulfilled its function in time, leads to transsexual existence. It had been primarily concerned with relationship: the experience, in marriage or celibacy as we have seen, of the deep-down appeal of love accompanied by the ambivalence of its successes and their insufficiency. Secondly, it had been a function of growth: since the world of the resurrection represents *fulfilled* humanity, reproduction has completed its role. In necessarily inadequate and insufficient language this is the content of Christ's response to the Sadducees. This short New Testament passage is of capital importance in grasping the meaning of sexuality within the Christian perspective of the destiny of the world.

The account of Christ's birth points in the same direction. The account belongs to faith because nothing can demonstrate that it is false or impossible. Like many merely human realities, it eludes scientific argumentation which can neither weaken nor confirm it. But if we take it as it is presented, its meaning absolutely agrees with the response to the Sadducees. In the unique marriage of Joseph and Mary there occurs the passage from human sexuality to absolute love, the action of God which enables the human condition to surpass itself.

Mary was born of an ordinary couple, the offspring of perfectly natural sexual relations between her parents. Clearly, this is not stated in the Scriptural texts but it is something nobody would contradict. It means that Mary was a woman and only a woman. But—and this is precisely the mystery—she is dispensed from human ambivalence, from "turning in on herself" or, more traditionally, from original sin.

She was betrothed to a man of her tribe named Joseph. We are historically justified in thinking that, like every Israelite girl, she hoped to be the mother of the expected Messiah, a real yet very mysterious figure who was to be at once king, priest, and faithful servant, very human yet somehow transcendent. She learns from God that she is to be pregnant with a son who will be the Messiah. Her first reaction is astonishment: she "does not know man." The response she receives is couched with a depth that is peculiar to the Scriptures: this will be the work of God. For her there can be no further question, and she gives her consent.

Joseph also reacts. Matthew (1:18) tell us that "before they had lived together" Mary was found to be pregnant. As Joseph was a just man and did not wish to denounce her, he resolved to put her aside secretly. In his turn, he also is informed of the real nature of what is taking place, and his faith is solicited. We can remark in passing, it seems, that this version of the fact was certainly much more believable than what had naturally first come to his mind—as paradoxical as that may seem. In his turn, he also accepts.

A child who is God, incarnate in time and in the human condition, is going to be born in the most ordinary obstetric manner—embryonic growth, delivery, further growth. But he has not come from human sexuality as such; he arises directly from God, being himself God.

From then on, for this unique couple the specific function of sexuality has no more meaning. This couple is the tangible manifestation in time and history of the kingdom of God. Their life will be *sexed* but will have passed beyond the *sexual*.

This is the whole profound meaning of this mysterious affirmation—so offensive to certain minds—of Mary's virginity "before, during, and after childbirth," according to the traditional expression. She is wife and mother but has already passed beyond the temporal level of exercised sexuality.

In this context, celibacy lived in terms of the Christian conception of sexuality takes on a very precise and literally mystical significance: it sees life in terms of a mystery. A particular man or woman chooses—we have seen that this choice is possible—at some particular point to bear witness from then on to the transcendent mode of love proper to the world of the resurrection. Clearly, this can happen only if one is a believing Christian. Granting that, such belief can be a very powerful motivation for *positive* celibacy.

Certainly, when such motivation is distorted to any degree, it may be only an alibi for negative celibacy that arises out of neurosis—indeed, it may be nothing more than an alibi. But frequent clinical experience demonstrates that celibacy in which we discern negative elements affecting an individual's sexual maturity can be utilized quite positively, thanks to this motivation of faith, if it is lived authentically. There is a major difference between a neurotic woman who identifies with the Blessed Virgin and a woman who renounces emotional and sexual fulfillment in expectation of life outside of time and does not make this renunciation a kind of retrogressive recuperation. Leaving aside the personal option of faith, the clinical or psychological observer can establish the fact that there are cases of positive celibacy which are religiously motivated and cases of negative celibacy which have been harmoniously inserted into this context.

At this point it is necessary to recall that celibacy as a state of life is necessarily subject to change. The individual involved is not fixed once and for all in a particular attitude which does not allow any new problems. There can be crises, moments of doubt, stages of development, just as in marriage. These changes will vary according to whether the individual's emotional situation fits under what we have called positive or negative celibacy. In any case, changes will take place. There are high points in the life of every individual. There are moments when he perceives—not just intellectually but in a profound emotional experience—freedom from the frustrations he is normally obliged to accept.

As I am finishing a meal prior to an important appointment, I find myself facing a bowl of oranges. After a quick look I choose one of them. If I remain indecisive indefinitely, not only shall I not get an orange at all but I shall miss my appointment. So I choose *one*. In a very real sense, this means that *I deprive myself of the others*—but I nevertheless register the sight of them in my interior world at the moment of choice. During the day, on the occasion of some annoyance or dissatisfaction, there may come back to me the bothersome image of one or another of the oranges I did not take in order to choose the one I did. The oranges have become a privation for me, something now impossible to achieve. Will my disappointment be intense enough to immobilize me at least for the moment that it manifests itself?

This, of course, is only a trivial comparison. Celibacy

constitutes a much more fundamental frustration than being deprived of oranges. But we must also point out that it does permit commitments, accomplishments, distractions, and even joys which marriage does not allow. This fact is the theme of many old jokes and songs—"No cares have I to grieve me, No pretty little wife to deceive me, I'm as happy as a king, believe me. . . ."[2] Marriage also entails frustration.

In general terms, the question is very simple; but it is sometimes very complex and difficult to apply practically. Frustration can be borne only to the degree that one lives *positively* within the limits it imposes. This may be very simple in a case of positive celibacy since in a way this is its definition. Not that there will not be sorrowful times in the life of the positive celibate; but they will be only sorrowful, not paralyzing. It is a different case altogether with certain kinds of negative celibacy. But here there can be no general rules because each individual situation is conditioned differently.

When the frustration is imposed antecedently, consciously or unconsciously, it then becomes a matter of compensating in some way that is positive and valid for the individual concerned. This is where crises occur. At certain times during life these compensations appear inexplicably deceptive and the frustration cries out starkly. At thirty one's solitude will suddenly seem intolerable. At forty-five a man will suffer intensely because he has no

[2] It is a funny thing that no song says, "No care have I to grieve me, No handsome little husband to deceive me, I'm as happy as a Queen, believe me. . . ."

children. A woman will feel her deprivation of motherhood more continually but she may have periods of acute bitterness as menopause approaches.

There is no possibility of offering a general solution for these crises, as if a psychologist had some kind of superior, magical knowledge. However, I would like to point out one thing in terms of an allegory we have used before.

Someone afflicted with polio in youth had to renounce the profession he had chosen. But, thanks to this crisis, he was enabled to acquire a degree of culture, to achieve existential discoveries and levels of reflection which he would otherwise never have reached. There will be moments during his life when he will realize his frustrations very intensely. The compensations and enrichment that have been allowed him will appear worthless at such a price. But if this enrichment is real and has been translated into personal relationships—through his work, friendships, responsibilities, etc.—then these will only be bad moments. Without even explaining it to himself, he will wait until they pass because he will retain a basic sense of his own personal worth.

It is somewhat the same with the positive celibate. To the degree that he is able to compensate for his celibacy in a framework of human relationships where he feels secure of his position, the inevitable crises will be surmountable. Once again, it is useful to stress that married life is as subject to these crises as celibacy. But we see only our own crises and inevitably become incapable of imagining those of others. If celibates experience periods of regret or rebellion, they should think of the man who chose the orange. Having no orange at all may cause no more unhappiness than having chosen one and at the same time having to admit that one should have chosen another.

IV

INSTITUTIONAL CELIBACY

8. ECCLESIAL CELIBACY

A NUMBER OF INSTITUTIONS are so designed that an individual who wishes to belong to them must remain celibate. This is a distinct type of celibacy because it is the authoritative third party who demands that the individual, in exhange for a particular position, *not* express marital consent. Or this third party accepts the assurance that the individual will not express it for so long as he remains part of this particular, recognized institution. This constitutes a true contract between the particular society and the individual. The society says: "You wish to perform a particular activity within my organization; agreed, but I demand that you not marry." Or it declares: "I claim the right to be an organized institution constituted of celibates."

In the contemporary western world institutional celibacy which is not religiously oriented is rare and temporary. Certain professions for which celibacy is an explicit condition bind their members on a temporary basis.[1] Certain special military corps accept only unmarried volunteers who enlist for a limited time.

[1] Airline hostesses, for example; or certain classes of persons employed overseas by oil companies.

In our modern western civilization the only definitive institutional celibacy is religious. We must grasp that there are two kinds of societies. The Church is a universal and mystical society which totally transcends the context of civil societies or states. But its necessary and visible organized structure is co-terminous with them. In most western countries, with the separation of Church and State, the state accords the Church the right to organize within the state's territory according to its own norms, with the tacit agreement that this state will not, theoretically at least, concern itself with the Church organization. In exchange, the state does not accept the presence of the Church in civil affairs.

However it may be organized, definitive institutional celibacy exists only in relationship to the Church. In terms of the individuals concerned, there are two very different aspects. First there is religious or "regular" celibacy. Second there is ecclesiastical celibacy. These two aspects demand closer examination for the benefit of the reader, whether he belongs to the Church or not. We shall not adopt a dogmatic point of view. The relative value and legitimacy of these two states of life do not enter our discussion. De facto they exist. We have seen that celibacy is not necessarily an aberration nor an unhuman situation. Our viewpoint will be exclusively psychological and our only intentions will be to define the motivations for these two kinds of celibacy and the specific problems they present.

RELIGIOUS CELIBACY

Religious celibacy concerns groups of men or women organized according to a rule and constitutions which set forth a form of communal life which can vary greatly in its style and activities. The principle of these groups is the desire for a life consecrated to God. This kind of consecrated life is found in almost all religions. Within the Christian religion one of the roots of the monastic life lay in the desire to bear extraordinary witness of fidelity to Christ and in this way to continue to give testimony about him to the world by some means other than martyrdom, which became very rare after Constantine terminated the persecutions.

Those who enter such groups intend to commit themselves to a form of life which gives to the world visible witness concerning the resurrection of Christ through the renunciation of certain values of temporal life. Clearly, one of these values is sexual fulfillment. The religious specifically seeks this renunciation rather than the ministry of the Christian priesthood. In other words, one of the primary goals of the men or women who enter religion is *sexual continence*, the nonexercise of their sexuality. This goal is sought precisely in terms of the mystical motivation for celibacy that we examined above.

Terminology is important here. We speak of the "vow of chastity" but the expression is not exact. According to St. Thomas Aquinas, chastity is the virtue which, arising from temperance, governs the individual's harmonious conduct of his sexual life. Therefore, married people are not in any way excluded from the practice of this virtue. Chastity is a *positive*, not a privative, notion regarding sexuality. But since religious make a vow to *deprive* themselves of sexual activity, it would be more accurate to say that they make a vow of sexual continence. Since, from the Christian viewpoint, sexuality is worthily exercised only in marriage, they must necessarily remain celibate. Continence and celibacy as such are *directly* willed.

It is clear that for women there is no connection between this basic intention and the priesthood. Neither is there necessarily one in the case of men. The original communities founded by St. Benedict and his successors included only those few priests needed for the ministry and these were clearly reminded not to consider themselves superior to the other members. Only late in history were congregations established with a view to some particular type of priestly ministry. This happened under the pressure of changed social and religious circumstances. The Order of St. Dominic and the Society of Jesus are typical examples. This development caused a certain confusion between the commitment to the religious life and that to the priestly ministry.

Religious communities come in almost infinite variety with more or less ancient traditions which have in some cases been accumulated over the years and sometimes end by being burdensome: details of garb, exterior behavior, "ritual" terminology. But the basic principle is always the same: the three vows of sexual continence, nonpossession of personal property, and obedience—with great variations in terms of practice. This juridical structure which includes sexual continence is viewed as the means to a particular spiritual achievement. But Church authority can relieve an individual even of his perpetual vows if he requests it for serious reasons.

We also speak of a private vow which means that an individual binds himself alone and in secrecy to sexual continence. He may do this in the privacy of his relationship to a spiritual director. Such an action is very imprecise juridically. It is also very questionable psychologically. That a young person—usually a young girl—has a negative attitude both toward ordinary communal religious life and toward marriage poses an *a priori* question regarding a probable underlying psychological problem. Commitment to communal religious life is not abnormal even though it may be unusual. To view it only from the human side, both present-day observation and historical evidence indicate that a good number of people find quite satisfactory fulfillment and self-realization in this commitment, provided its motives are not clearly neurotic.

ECCLESIASTICAL CELIBACY

The other aspect of this question is in a sense the inverse of what we have just been discussing. In the western Catholic Church an individual who wishes to be a priest commits himself to an "ecclesiastical" organization which imposes on him the condition of promising celibacy when he reaches the order of subdeacon.[2]

[2] The three major orders are subdiaconate, diaconate, and priesthood. The fact that Vatican II studied the possibility of married

The individual directly wills the priesthood. Under the prevailing conditions of the western Catholic Church he can reach it only by promising not to marry. As a logical consequence, his Christian concern for the virtue of chastity obliges him to sexual continence. But in this case celibacy and continence are not the object of his commitment. They are accepted as the marginal consequence of a quite distinct commitment to the priesthood.

It may be useful to recall—or explain—to the reader the exact nature of this commitment. A man who wishes to be a priest in the Catholic religion asks to be the voluntary instrument of Christ in terms of the signs of his presence which he has instituted, namely, the sacraments. These culminate and are rooted in the outstanding sign, the Mass, which is the making present of the sacrificial meal which Christ had with his Apostles on the eve of his Passion.

The priest presides over the prayer of the assembly of believers. He announces the Word and offers the Sacrifice. The Christian priesthood is a *function* which we can call "mysteric" since it expresses the mystery of our redemptive relationship to Christ. This is the essential nature of the priestly commitment. The law of ecclesiastical celibacy connected with this priestly function clearly poses a number of questions.

At the present time a solemn promise of celibacy is made to the bishop who confers the subdiaconate. Ac-

---

deacons indicates that we are dealing with a changeable ecclesiastical law.

cording to the laws of the ecclesiastical society this promise means that if the priest later marries, his marriage is null with all the juridical consequences which that involves. This leads to quite paradoxical situations: a priest who marries civilly is considered unmarried by ecclesiastical society and, indeed, as subject to sanctions; on the other hand, he is quite validly married in the eyes of civil society and all the various public organisms with which he has dealings.

The first question to be resolved is whether celibacy was explicitly attached to the priesthood at its institution by Christ. This is an important question. If, by Christ's will, celibacy were part of the priestly commitment, certain sectors of the Catholic Oriental Church—and the whole of the Oriental Church separated from Rome—would be seriously betraying their founder. That this is not the case is beyond question.

Some authors have tried desperately to discover some foundation for the theory of a primitive origin of celibacy in a kind of law which was observed before being formulated. These authors[3] attempt to demonstrate an *a priori* position. In their opinion celibacy was explicitly connected with the priesthood; or, if not, it was implicitly accepted from the time of Christ or at least the Apostles and was observed by those who knew the historic Christ. Their mental gymnastics in the interpretation of texts is somewhat touching because it shows great good will. But such argumentation could not be employed now. Serious

[3] For example, see Vassal, *Le Célibat ecclésiastique au ler siècle de l'Eglise*, 1896.

historical studies over the past fifty years, at least, have demonstrated its inconsistencies.

Even in 1826 J. Bonicel had no difficulty in showing, in his *Considerations on the Celibacy of Priests*, that there is no trace of any such explicit or implicit law in the first centuries of the Church. Rigorous historical works demonstrate this fact beyond question. In *Etudes de critique et d'histoire religieuse*, which appeared in 1905, Vacandard dissipates all illusion and confusion on the question.

Indeed, it requires only a little reflection on the evangelical data to see clearly that the priesthood and celibacy are two entirely independent realities in the mind of Christ. According to traditional theology, the priesthood was instituted at the Last Supper: "Do this in memory of me." There is no question of anything else. Besides, Peter was married, as was evident from the fact that Christ had previously cured his mother-in-law of a fever. Later on, Paul describes to Timothy (2 Tim., 3:3) the ideal of a "bishop" as a "man of one wife."

In another place, and within a quite general context, Christ speaks of "voluntary eunuchs for the sake of the kingdom of heaven" (Matt., 19:10-12). It is evident that he is using a metaphor for continence, not for surgical castration. This teaching clearly designates what we have called religious or mystical celibacy. The precise institution of the priestly function is quite distinct from Christ's teaching on celibacy. As they come from the New Testament they are realities of two different orders.

In passing we should point out that the statement about

continence was provoked by an instruction about marriage. Christ had established the exclusiveness and indissolubility of the marital union: monogamy and fidelity. The disciples, therefore, conclude that it "is not profitable for a man to marry." Then, in the context of the value and demands of marriage, Christ discusses voluntary continence for the sake of the kingdom. Christ rarely spoke about the actual exercise of sexuality. For him it is evidently not the essential but only an aspect of human nature and its finality.

A thorough study of the history of the ecclesiastical law of celibacy would add very important elements to our reflection. Not being an historian, I cannot even give a rough treatment of it here. We shall limit ourselves to recalling in a schematic way the main lines of this historical development as they are found in works like that of Vacandard.

One initial remark is necessary. It would be a grave methodological error to approach a study like this with the implicit viewpoint of a return to the past. Failure to recognize normal human evolution represents just as false a rigidity as the unwillingness to modify still-observed customs and institutions of the recent past which are beginning to cause problems. To return to the use of oil lamps, because they were used in the catacombs, is just as foolish as to refuse to move beyond the gas lamp of the last century.

From our psychological point of view, it would certainly be an error to consider that the manner in which ecclesiastical celibacy was conceived in the second and third centuries was the norm to which we must return. The development of a positive law is significant in terms of the evolution of a collective consciousness. If it runs the unquestionable risk of becoming rigidly fixed, it also expresses a deepening of understanding. Not to recognize this would be to fail to recognize a constant element of individual and collective psychological evolution. It would be the same error as to deny that this law can be modified and evolve. This attitude automatically provokes psychological conflicts in individuals caught between the law whose spirit is insufficiently profound and concrete conditions of knowledge and existence which have progressed considerably.

A connection between the priestly ministry and a certain ideal of sexual life developed very early. For example, the priesthood, or more exactly, its full expression, the espiscopate, was compatible only with monogamy, as Paul said to Timothy. This monogamy did not only mean having but one wife at a time but having only one during one's lifetime. A remarried widower could not be a bishop.

At the beginning of the third century Tertullian argues strongly against the remarriage of priests. However, his argumentation rests on a conception of sexuality which is implicitly pejorative. Gradually the ideal of non-remarriage evolved toward the ideal of celibacy, but not in an institutional or obligatory form. This is how St. Epiphanius expresses it in the fourth century. On the other hand, Clement of Alexandria, in the beginning of the third century, clearly affirms the priest's right to "use marriage" if he is married. So, clearly, he could be married.

It appears that the prohibition against married priests having sexual relations with their wives was formulated in the fourth century for the church of Rome. But in Gaul in the sixth century marriage for sacred ministers was the general custom, without any implication of weakness on their part.

A real tension was appearing more and more clearly between the tendency to impose celibacy and the realization of the various abuses to which this authoritarian obligation often leads in practice (concubinage, promiscuity, etc.). Certain periods were particularly troubled from this point of view. We must, however, take account of possible indignant exaggerations in those who discussed the problem.

The Council of Bourges, in 1031, for the first time explicitly formulated the decision to admit to the subdiaconate only individuals binding themselves to remain celibate. This marks a clear separation from the Oriental Church. The Latin Church, under the predominant influence of Rome, resolutely bound itself to legislation which has not changed since. In 1123 Calixtus II climaxed this legislation by declaring marriages contracted by clerics null and void.

This development did not occur with unanimous agreement or without controversies. Some argued against the obligation of celibacy on the grounds that it risked leading to grave moral disorders among clerics. It was easy to prove that a number of them, especially at certain periods, lived in concubinage and sometimes led truly scandalous lives. The Renaissance Papal Court offered many examples.

This tension has not been resolved. Ever since the eleventh century certain authors have asked whether this law, which obliges a man in so untouchable and personal an area, did not do more harm than good. Passionate debates have sometimes taken place. Naturally, the partisans of both camps exaggerate and press their positions. For one group, the disorders which this law provokes are the general rule and constitute one of the Church's scandals. For the other, celibacy is the almost unique condition for clerical virtue. These latter often ignore or pretend to ignore facts of everyday observation.

9. REASONS FOR THE LAW OF CELIBACY

It would be pretentious to think that we could understand and explain fully all the factors which led to this legislation and have maintained it ever since. Nevertheless, on reflection we can single out some which seem beyond question.

The first and most important is undoubtedly the gradual awareness of the mystical significance of celibacy, as we tried to describe it. Simple meditation on the teaching of Christ and St. Paul as well as the influence of the first monastic movements led to this idea: celibacy which accompanies the priestly ministry seems *preferable* for it bears witness in time to the transsexual love of the world of the resurrection. But, if celibacy appears preferable, it is so *in itself*, that is, within a general conception of the human condition as perfected by revelation. It was not conceived as absolutely preferable and applicable to every person in terms of his moral and spiritual growth.

So far as we can see, this mystical value of voluntary celibacy was rapidly sensed very profoundly. This value was founded in faith, that is, it was transcendent in its significance and power. But it was defined as an option, as an "ideal," as St. Epiphanius expressed it. As it passed from this stage to a juridical obligation, many other factors played a part. The latter is a basically very different point of view which one rightfully reproaches with hiding or even falsifying the true value of celibacy.

Indisputably, a factor in this development was the *necessary* and gradual establishment of the "clergy," that is, a particular social class who needed to be powerful in order to save civilization when it was threatened. In its full development this was a social class formed by "clerks." The men who entered sacred orders were practically the only ones who knew how to read. They had a monopoly of culture and thought. The others, who did not know how to read and had so many other urgent things to do, were the "laity." It was normal that during periods as troubled as the centuries following the collapse of the Roman Empire, the clerics progressively tended to direct operations and to organize themselves in a coherent and powerful manner in order to strengthen their role.

There resulted that admirably balanced and stable structure that we call the "medieval Church"—an error of language, for it does not refer to the Church in the full sense but only to the organization of a particular social body which circumstances forced to be centered on the priesthood and its services. Total confusion between this temporal governing power and the mystical and pastoral ministry lasted for a long time. Is it totally and everywhere dissipated even now?, one may well ask.

One of the strengths of this social body was precisely that basic goods were not dispersed through inheritance. An organization of celibates clearly acquires greater cohesiveness and power from a financial point of view and in terms of the means of initiative, since nothing gets past it. Among the secular clergy spirituality tended toward celibacy which was the very foundation of the monastic communities. It is not unreasonable to conjecture that the need for organization and solidarity during troubled times contributed at least implicitly toward elevating into a law of the "ecclesiastical society" what would have appeared in other circumstances purely as a spiritual ideal.

As with every human reality the results were ambivalent. Without any doubt both groups of clergy made first-rank contributions to the formation of modern civilization. The present problem arose because, once this civilization became adult, it broke with the former structures, and the clergy as a directive social body no longer had a place as it once had.

On the other hand, abuses were unquestionable. Numerous men, like St. Bernard, reacted violently against them. Some monasteries had become veritable feudal fortresses and some bishops were potentates. The use of this power was not always directed to the benefit and betterment of the people who were governed. The moral decadence of the clergy during certain periods is an indisputable fact.

Besides, even if the *law* was observed, it very often happened that continence was not, and many priests lived in concubinage. Indeed, it seems that this did not pose many problems within their environment and did not always diminish their prestige and their authentically priestly influence. Human reality, as history shows, is not simple.

Undeniably, a negative attitude toward sexuality—and

hence, about marriage—played a part in this development. Despite the fact that several times in history the Church has condemned certain sects which presented sexuality as evil in itself,[1] there has always been an underlying tendency to consider everything connected with sexuality, including marriage, as at least suspect. The implicit presence in many subtle ways of this attitude, which we are obliged to call a taboo, made it very difficult to discern. Its influence was very powerful. It implicitly influenced the step to make celibacy obligatory because sexual activity, even in marriage, was viewed as essentially defiled. Certain authors—and not necessarily very ancient ones—have gone so far as to call sexual relations in marriage "permitted sins."

The influence of certain major authors of the first centuries clearly moved in this direction. This could happen quite easily because complete ignorance of the nature of sexuality prevailed then and for a long time afterward. Also, the millenarian taboo was always ready to revive under the guise of theological reasoning that bordered on heresy. Modern psychology makes us realize that sometimes some of these authors had personal neurotic problems which contributed to the dangerous exaggerations in their thinking.

In the 1950 number of *Etudes Carmélitaines*, entitled "Mysticism and Continence," there is a series of very valuable studies of this problem. Among others, a very

[1] For example, the Encratites (a name derived from the Greek word meaning continence); the Mersalians (who rapidly fell into worse disorders); the Cathars; etc.

well-researched and documented article by Dr. Charles A. Nodet shows how many of St. Jerome's positions on marriage may have been distorted by his own sexual repulsion. As an example of this kind of influence regarding celibacy, we shall cite here only a few particularly significant texts.

Regarding marriage, St. Jerome wrote: "You have learned in marriage itself all the problems it can present. For you it was like being filled with quail flesh to the point of nausea. Your throat felt the bitter bile; you rejected the sour and rotten food; your inflamed stomach began to feel better. Why do you want to take up again what has been so harmful to you? This would be acting like a dog who returns to his vomit or the pig who rolls in the mud immediately after having been washed." Regarding the desire for fecundity, he wrote: "As for marrying in order to have children, or so that the family name may not disappear, or in order to have support and heirs in one's old age, this is the height of stupidity." A husband can truly love his wife only outside of sexuality: "If one abstains from sexual union, one honors his wife; in the opposite case, it is clear that one injures her, for everything opposed to honor is an injury."

Tertullian seems to have been influenced by the Manichean doctrines that the body and its operations were the work of the "evil god." In his *Confessions* St. Augustine informs us that his emotional and sexual life was not well-balanced. He was not at ease with his sexual impulses which seem badly adjusted to a modern psychologist. His philosophical reflection on sexuality and marriage have clearly been affected by this condition, even though his teaching on marriage marks an important step forward historically. This sexual taboo, whose excesses official documents of the church several times denounced, remained unquestionably present. It is reflected in several schools of spirituality and even in works which are not so ancient.

There is nothing astonishing in this. Sexuality with all its manifestations is the most mysterious phenomenon in the world, intimately connected with the dialectic of life and death. It is an experience that has always been bound up with a religious or philosophic sense of awe. Scientific understanding of it is very recent. It is difficult for us to realize that the eminent men of the sixteenth century, like Leonardo da Vinci, were totally ignorant of sexual physiology, for example.

Philosophical and theological reflection was necessarily affected by this ignorance. The principal sources available to such reflection were the ancient authors, Greek and other philosophical trends, and certain modes of deductive reasoning. Science as such did not make its first timid appearance until the seventeenth century. The Galileo affair is one of the first manifestations of an absolutely new conflict: men begin to know the world through observation independent of philosophical traditions. Unquestionable assertions of this new kind of knowledge might contradict accepted ideas, open up new perspectives for reflection, and question older systems of thought. Above all, they might displace the sense of mystery by replacing more or less magical "beliefs" with learned certitudes. One can no longer take thunder for the voice of the divinity when one knows it to be an electrical phenomenon.

In every area—cosmology, physics, chemistry, etc.—scientific knowledge is a recent fact. Its definitive birth and prodigious development scarcely date back a century and a half. Human sexuality has only been scientifically examined for this same length of time. Until modern times, for example, there was complete ignorance about the physiology of the sexual glands. It was not known that the woman, through the process of ovulation, had an *active* part in fertility. She was considered only a passive receptacle charged with caring for the only thing that had any importance—what the man deposited in her. There was total ignorance of the tremendous wastage in spermatogenesis, and the sperm was considered as a sacred liquor. One was equally ignorant of the mechanism of erection, the formation of the sperm, menstruation. The same was true of the very complex interactions of hormonal secretions. Above all, there was ignorance of what modern psychology, inaugurated by Freud's discoveries, has revealed in terms of an evolving, dynamic, and personal conception of the emotional life and sexuality.

It is curious that this medical ignorance combined with prejudices directly rooted in the millenarian taboo. For example, clinical observation should have been able long ago to show that the masturbation of adolescence was a banal matter of no practical consequence for a person's health. But this evidence was not seen. Medical works of the seventeenth century are astonishing—and humorous.

All these discoveries completely overturn earlier ideas

about sexuality and its meaning. They bring out its positive value, they exorcise archaic fears. They lead us to grasp demands of moral behavior which are much more elevated, more *human*—we could very exactly say, more authentically spiritualized. It is not exaggerated to say that our time is marked by the discovery of the true meaning of the marital relationship and its real value. Advances in the theology of marriage are one example.

A conception of marriage and celibacy still more or less conditioned by prescientific taboos is no longer acceptable. It would be a grave error to argue about celibacy, for example, on the basis of ancient authors whose authority and intellectual power may be considerable, but who were almost completely ignorant about sexuality. The problem is analogous to that posed by other scientific discoveries: cosmology, biological evolution, the structure of matter.

Even a man like St. Thomas Aquinas was necessarily subject to what we may very precisely call the "nonscience" of his time. His language is now insufficient. In other words, if he were living now, he would think the same fundamental truths but in a more profound, better documented fashion. He would certainly express them in a very different way. One can no longer base an apology for celibacy on an underestimation of the value of sexuality, as St. Jerome implicitly did.

The ecclesiastical law of the Latin Church which obliges priests to bind themselves to celibacy has always been a problem. St. Bernard seems to have been reticent on the subject. It is no secret that it is presently being called into question. The discussion very often becomes impassioned: some still perceive the influence of the taboo, and others perceive its opposite, the anti-taboo. Some cry out, without reflection or distinctions, "Priests should marry." Others answer, "Never! The law of celibacy is untouchable." The latter contention is false historically and in principle. It often translates a secret wish *not to face* the sometimes dramatic problems which this law, dating in its present form from the eleventh century, actually poses.

When priestly celibacy is criticized in principle, one must not be duped into accepting a false level on which the criticism may be placed. In the light of modern anthropology celibacy is not necessarily an abnormal situation nor necessarily the cause of an unhuman life, as long as it is not the symptom of a major neurosis. Criticism which contends that it is abnormal is actually an alibi for those who formulate it. The real question is something quite different.

Observe closely those who say that the celibacy of priests is abnormal and must cease. They are personalities whom it disturbs, at least unconsciously. That there are men who accept celibacy as a legal obligation and a matter of possible normality makes them question and experience anguish about their own inferiority. This arises from their sexual immaturity, especially when it is not clearly perceived. In other words, those who perceive that celibates are effectively frustrated in their emotional life may be intolerably confronted with their own incapacity to master their instincts.

This is a very realistic and very profound element of the psychology of the critics. Prolonged adolescence can hardly bear the sight and company of a better adjusted adult. Gide needed to persuade himself that all people of value were homosexual and to draw as many young men as possible into his perverse esthetic world in order to be less alone with the insupportable anguish of his neurotic anomaly.

Some reasons why a priest might be celibate are not easily dismissed. The first and most important is what we called mystical motivation: a man who commits himself to the priesthood chooses to commit himself also to bear witness to the transsexual world of the resurrection. Christ was celibate, but we must not forget that he was God and we are not.

Practical reasons are also put forward, and they are indisputable: greater availability, the secrecy of the confessional. But they also imply the indisputable disadvantages: lessened understanding of human problems, the danger of "old maidism," authoritarian compensation.

The relatively calm reflections which have appeared in the last several years have not focused precisely on the celibacy of priests. Their concern has been the ecclesiastical law which, since it imposes celibacy absolutely, makes it not a personal option but an external administrative condition to which one must consent, willingly or not. The excessively juridical manner in which this law has been administered has also been subject to discussion. Even when a priest evidenced real psychological incapacity for sexual continence, his bishop could obtain for him until recently only a reduction to the lay state without the right to marry. This was cleary the height of absurdity. A good number of insoluble crises were created by this attitude. There have even been suicides. Such administrative blindness is certainly accounted for by an underlying sexual taboo, as some of the documents attest.

For the past several years, especially since the confrontation of Vatican II, ecclesiastical celibacy has been publicly debated. This has inevitably created new psychological conditions for those who live it or are called to live it. We must try to understand them.

For the past twenty years especially, sexuality has been an everyday matter—not just in the form of bawdy stories but in terms of both physiological and psychological scientific knowledge and research. This profound change of climate is irreversible. The not always well-conceived popularization of psychoanalytic notions about sexuality has raised quite novel questions for a clergy which was on the whole very badly prepared. A certain number of priests and young men studying for the priesthood have been deeply troubled by them. Nowadays everyone talks about repression, emotional evolution, maturity, unconscious motivations. Formerly, everything was simple: a young man decided on the priesthood, which meant celibacy, as he realized—and "grace would help him," as was commonly said.

Now science comes along to question this apparent simplicity. Certain sectors of the Church energetically fought this questioning, as did certain medical groups for the same kind of reason: psychoanalysis, which had its startling birth in the nineteenth century, disclosed a very different anthropology from that of classical organicist medicine. A striking example of this is that the Council, which intended to contact the modern world, practically ignored the anthropology of Freud, which had already changed many areas of knowledge and activity.

Reactions to this changed climate have been very diverse among priests and seminarians. Among them have been: a categorical rejection of any kind of psychology—this represents an easily explained defense against unbearable questioning; an eager grasp of arguments culled from a few books to justify leaving the Church by marrying; the sudden uncovering of deep unrest. This last reaction is the most common. Men already committed, or on their way toward commitment, have turned to modern psychology to find help in resolving their uneasiness. Two examples will clarify this point better than any theoretical exposition.

X, twenty-three-years-old, entered the minor seminary at about twelve and went on to the major seminary at the end of his college studies. He performed his military service, although his duty was influenced by his being a seminarian, and then returned to his studies. He becomes inwardly troubled to the degree that his spiritual director advises him to see a psychiatrist. His problem is that he realizes that he has never *personally* posed to himself the question of his emotional fulfillment and has not resolved the problem of celibacy *for himself*. On the advice of the psychiatrist and with agreement of his director, he takes a leave from the seminary in order to live for two or three years like any unmarried man of his age, working and earning a living in normal circumstances. This also gives him the opportunity to consult the psychiatrist regularly as he assumes for himself the responsibility of his personal development. At the end of two years he comes to a lucid and peaceful decision, reenters the seminary, and moves on to the priesthood. This time his attitude is entirely different because he has sorted out for himself the matter of the priestly ministry and the condition of celibacy which Church law imposes on him.

Y, forty-years-old, a priest for fifteen years, has experienced a deep unease ever since his ordination and despite himself has looked for emotional compensations. Finally, he sees clearly that he has let himself be committed in a direction that he has never *willed* but which he accepted under the implicit and constant pressure of a very clerical family atmosphere. Several times he tried to oppose this pressure. He found no one to help him—just the opposite, in fact—in the seminary where he was and where nobody understood his disturbance. As a result, he just let things take their course and accepted a life of celibacy and a vocation which he never positively chose. When the tension became intolerable he appealed to a psychologist. He was able to face the reality of his problem and to assume, without rebellion, the responsibility of rejecting an imposed celibacy and asking to be relieved of the obligations which he had never in fact chosen.

It is perhaps a little simplistic—but not basically inexact—to say that these two cases would have been resolved completely differently before modern psychological insights had entered our explicit preoccupations. X would perhaps never have become a priest. Y would perhaps have unfrocked himself in a negative revolt, with all that can represent in terms of human and spiritual destruction.

The conditions under which celibacy is presented have considerable importance for the profound psychological attitude of candidates for the priesthood. Under present conditions priesthood and celibacy are absolutely and definitively bound together. Independently of the mystical motivation that we discussed, the psychological approach is defined in one way or another as nonmarriage.

For a boy of eighteen or nineteen or even older, whose emotional development has been very disturbed in terms of sexual maturity, this may offer the ideal way to justify his incapacity for the commitment of marriage. This will not take place through conscious and reasoned calculation but as an unconscious solution for a conflict which he does not even perceive. Authentic religious motivation may also be present, but there is a great risk that it also may be more or less distorted. It also may be only an unconscious alibi, even though expressed in all sincerity.

There can be no pretense that this is not a frequent case. In the modern western world the Catholic ecclesiastical state is the only instutition professing institutional and definitive celibacy. It is not astonishing that it attracts a certain number of individuals who are in difficulty. Quite sincerely they may find it a solution which gives some meaning to their sexual immaturity or even to their neuroses. It is well known that the proportion of candidates of this type for the ecclesiastical state is higher than for any other career. This is particularly true of more or less conscious homosexuals.

Still within the framework of a psychological discussion, another quite different remark is called for. The fact that the law of ecclesiastical celibacy is being publicly questioned forcibly changes the climate. It does not always add clarification. Many publications have proposed that there be married priests, which would be theoretically quite possible as we have seen.

This does not simplify things for men who are already priests and are having difficulties in adjusting to their celibacy. In the back of their minds they may have the confused and unformulated hope that some day they will be able to marry and still remain priests. This seems scarcely possible at this time. This kind of confused and illusory hope is no help to them. It only feeds their uneasiness and intensifies their rejection of celibacy. For some of them the problem could perhaps be solved by consultations with the right persons and by more enlightened understanding on the part of ecclesiastical authorities.

On the other hand, a systematic refusal to raise the question would also only complicate the problem. Some find themselves emotionally trapped in a contradictory situation, feeling deeply the essential nonidentity of priesthood and celibacy and, at the same time, deeply offended that others stubbornly refuse to reflect on the question.

The decision of Paul VI on this problem contributed

toward the relaxation of this conflict. He demanded that the Fathers of the Council not debate this problem publicly but that all questions concerning it be addressed to him. In this way the confusion of a discussion by a large group was avoided in order to promote a methodical study by small committees. This was the only attitude capable of reducing as much as possible the psychological tension provoked over the past several years.

Clinical experience can discern a definite evolution. Formerly a priest like Y in our case faced the prospect that his insolubly dramatic personal problem would not be recognized by the Roman authorities. The psychological consequences were often serious: bitterness, belligerence, and despair which hindered psychological and spiritual development. We know that now this attitude of anonymous and automatic refusal has been profoundly changed. The situation of the individual in difficulty is freed of these burdens. He knows implicitly that he has a chance of being heard and perhaps of being able to leave the priesthood honorably and to marry as a Christian. The belligerence against the Church which was sometimes very violent a few years ago no longer has much to feed on. It is also less difficult to demonstrate to certain individuals that with them this aggressiveness is only a psychological alibi.

Another remark is also called for. The public discussion of the various aspects of priestly celibacy likewise changes the climate in which young men envisage the problem. The properly supernatural dimension of the priesthood is now more explicitly perceived among the young. Specialists in vocations, as little attentive to the reality of what is happening as they are, notice that more and more young men are attracted by the priesthood perceived and categorized very objectively but that they do not accept systematic celibacy. So far as one can judge, it seems that quite a large number of young Christians abandon the idea of priestly commitment for this reason. This is a quite new psychological fact. Perhaps it was implicit formerly; the novelty is that it has been explicitly stated in the past few years.

It is very important to realize that it is not priestly celibacy which is being argued but only the way in which an ecclesiastical law, which dates from the eleventh century, conceives and presents it. This questioning may be variously explained. One of the most important reasons—although still very confusedly perceived—is the radical change in the structures of western civilization. In the debates which surround the question of religious liberty it is this change which is in fact revealed. To take only the example of France, until 1789 the clergy were one of the powers of the state. This created a climate of which we have no idea. A doctor who did not call a priest to the bedside of a dying person was liable to judicial prosecution. The Chevalier de la Barre was condemned to death for having refused to genuflect when a procession was passing. The sorrowful remembrance of religious persecution, still so alive in the Cévennes, is another example of the solidarity of royal power with the Catholic clergy.

We must see that facts of this kind, which appear literally odious to a modern Christian conscience, express the *end* of a very ancient system and the drama of its breakdown. In the high Middle Ages it was basically necessary that a strong structure and extensive temporal power belong to the ecclesiastical organization. Western civilization was enabled to establish itself and develop from this starting-point.

In the course of centuries, especially starting with the end of the Middle Ages and the Renaissance, culture, thought, and the capability of managing affairs were no longer the exclusive possession of the clerics. Gradually nonclerics grew conscious of their own possibilities and role. A distinction between the temporal power and the spiritual power was made more and more.

By the seventeenth century a Canossa was no longer possible. Louis XIV did not owe his crown to the Pope. But he was still very strongly influenced by Bossuet–for example, in the matter of persecuting religious dissent. The climate was such that even Napoleon wished to be annointed by the Pope. The disappearance of the truly political power of the Sovereign Pontiff dates only from 1870. In France the legal rupture with clericalism, that is, the clear distinction between the political power of the state and the apostolic mission of the Church, was only possible after 1901.

In modern times the clergy is no longer a part of the state nor is it a social and administrative power. It is a body of men organized hierarchically for a task quite free of confusion: to announce visibly the kingdom of heaven in Christ in and beyond time. That the structures of the clergy are still those of the *ancien régime* and that a certain nostalgia for past power remains causes the great problem in the evolution called for by the Second Vatican Council.

Institutional and obligatory celibacy—the content of ecclesiastical law—was certainly one of the strengths of the clergy of former times in the necessary role it had to fulfill. Now that this role of temporal authority no longer belongs to it—which liberates and augments its spiritual role and its power to shoulder that role—we can ask whether the celibacy of the priest could not be made more profound as a true spiritual sign of a personal option. It is clearly not up to us to settle the question. We can only contribute to framing it from the point of view of the psychological realities which clinical experience reveals.[2]

Another reason helps explain the present questioning of

[2] From this viewpoint it is interesting to note what the Vatican II decrees state regarding the celibacy of priests. First, the document *Lumen gentium* establishes the possibility of the principle of conferring the diaconate on mature married men. Secondly, the decree *Presbyterum ordinis* declares: "The practice of perfect and perpetual continence for the sake of the kingdom of heaven has been recommended by Christ the Lord; all through the centuries and in our days also many Christians have accepted it joyfully and have practiced it without reproach. The Church has held it in high esteem particularly for the priestly life. . . . Certainly it is not demanded by the nature of the priesthood, as the practice of the primitive Church and the tradition of the Oriental Churches show." The general lines of this text clearly surpasses the limits of pure legalism. The decree *Optatam totius ecclesiae renovationem* declares: "Seminarians who, according to the holy and firm laws of their own rite, observe the venerable tradition of priestly celibacy. . . ." This text follows the same direction.

the law of celibacy. It is a corollary of the preceding reason. Positive celibacy, which permits satisfactory personal fulfillment from the human point of view, demands a certain minimum of emotional maturity. Its psychological demands are the same as those of marriage, as paradoxical as that may appear. One must be as adult and as capable of sexed relationships to be a good positive celibate as to be a good husband and father.

The very conception and style of the complex system of the recruiting and formation of priests dates from an earlier point of view and includes much of what is regressive from the disturbed nineteenth century. There is now general and even official questioning of this system, after some experiments and initiatives were sometimes stifled by Roman authority.

The human educative value of a family atmosphere in which a child has experienced what is called a vocation is often very questionable. The desire to be a priest—this is the only psychologically acceptable expression—which a boy of ten years of age may express can contain various emotional elements. Not rarely a boy may quite sincerely express in this way his *unconscious* reaction to his mother's *unconscious* desire not to see him marry—anybody else, that is.

Clinical findings sometimes give us pause. In an important French seminary a specialist who conducted psychological examinations ascertained that seventy per cent of the young men—median age of twenty-one—had no father psychologically speaking, a widowed mother, a weak father who was hardly "present," or a sick and infirm father. It is evident that the prospect of celibacy cannot be realistically conceived when a man knows that if he becomes a priest, he will not be able to marry. The emotional crisis that marks the time of puberty can sometimes provoke a more or less permanent withdrawal from the prospect of committing oneself to marriage. A "vocation" that appears for the first time around the age of fourteen or fifteen always bothers an alert psychologist, because it is quite probable that it expresses some underlying problem.

Minor seminaries have been and still are subject to strong criticism. Great effort is being made to neutralize these criticisms which were often completely justified. For a long time the archaic rules of minor seminaries turned them into homes where young men preparing for the priesthood were treated like children and lived completely shut off from reality. Here also great efforts have been quite effectively made to change the atmosphere. But until recently it frequently happened that a boy of ten or eleven entered the mold of a formation in which everything combined to keep him from ever achieving normal *sexed* relationships. He was prepared for celibacy in an atmosphere which tried to keep him in a stage of prepuberty. The anecdotes—unfortunately true—about this atmosphere are plentiful.

Usually things go along somehow or other, with crises and difficulties that could certainly have been avoided. But real disasters were not—and are not—rare. The psychological crisis of adolescence, delayed by all these factors in the family and in education, can explode around thirty and then everything is questioned—too late. To put it very generally, it was as if one imposed celibacy in advance on young men who were formed in such a manner that they would have the greatest possible difficulty later on. Such a statement may seem excessive; it is only a slightly forced summary of what was occurring generally fifteen or twenty years ago and is still happening today in some places.

The excessive frequency of these subsequent difficulties, or even catastrophes, caused a good number of those in responsible positions to reflect and pose the questions clearly. We must not paint too black a picture. The difficulties and catastrophes do not represent the majority. This is a cause for surprise when we reflect on the unbelievable ineptitude of these educative procedures. This proves on the one hand that everything cannot be reduced to psychology. On the other hand it proves that we cannot mathematically explore in advance the human personality's resources of adaptation and development, which are often richer than we could suppose. But the minority represented by bad development—neuroses, abandonment of the priesthood, etc.—appeared too large to those responsible and to the specialists they consulted. It called for a general questioning of the human quality of this style of formation.[3]

Priestly celibacy is humanly possible, but it cannot have any human or spiritual value unless it is a harmonious *personal* utilization of a negative celibacy—a very frequent case—or better, a positive celibacy. One is right

[3] The Vatican II decree, *Optatam totius ecclesiae renovationem*, cited above, officially confirms this effort.

to ask whether, in this new world of ours, the ecclesiastical law making it obligatory and juridical does not place it in an archaic framework. One is also right to ask whether this point of view does not in fact sap its value and mask its authentic spiritual significance.

Theologically speaking, celibacy is not a part of the priesthood in itself. It is not demanded for the priestly function. Its meaning is much more profound than that of a legal condition. To be humanly positive, this kind of celibacy must be experienced as an interpersonal fulfillment which goes beyond the sexual–and beyond the juridical order as well. It must be related to the "kingdom of the resurrection," but also to the human community to which the individual consecrates his activity. Concrete situations differ very much. There is a certain conception of the episcopate which expresses this relationship very well: the bishop is the spouse of his territorial Church as Christ is the spouse of the universal Church.

Priestly celibacy is humanly possible from a psychological and medical point of view, but the data of modern anthropology show that it demands certain conditions: sufficient emotional maturity, a realistic and positively supernatural motivation which is not an alibi for a neurotic rejection or fear of sexuality. Theologians stress that in the mystery of his grace God helps individuals to bear the situation in which they are placed; this is a reality of a different order from the scientific. It has no place in this study. We limit ourselves here to the study of the human side of the problem.

Nevertheless, it appears desirable, from the point of

view of psychology and mental hygiene, that the juridical and external aspect of ecclesiastical celibacy not jeopardize what we have called its mystical motivation. In our world it is indispensable that the Church assure the free and personal character of ecclesiastical celibacy and take into account the progress made in understanding human behavior.

CONCLUSION

WE OFTEN HEAR IT SAID about a person who is not well balanced that "it isn't surprising: he is unmarried." There is an implicit current conviction that celibacy makes people a little odd, that it provokes repressions, that it embitters a person, etc. Attentive observation of the facts shows this implicit conviction to be false and oversimplified. Part of the reason is a very common phenomenon: we really only notice the things that go wrong and forget to think of the many things that go smoothly. We are struck by an air crash and forget about all the airplanes that do not have accidents. This is an instinctive reaction which is most remarkable when experienced within a large group. Its psychological foundations would be interesting to examine.

In this way we notice those unmarried persons who are unbalanced and we do not pay attention at the same time to the well-balanced celibates around us or to the married persons who are unbalanced. A hasty and false assigning of a cause to the effect establishes a connection between celibacy and emotional lack of balance.

In fact, the case is really just the contrary, as we tried to show in the first part of our clinical examination. Usually celibacy, continent or not, in disturbed persons is a consequence or sign of a badly developed or neurotic personal emotional situation. It is one symptom among others of this situation. It is the lack of balance which causes the celibacy.

We saw that, more often than one thinks, such situations are more or less fully compensated and that many negative celibates manage to achieve a satisfactory balance in their lives. Naturally it can happen that celibacy and its resultant frustration may aggravate the underlying neurosis. This depends on many variable factors: the person's environment, the nature of the problem, etc.

Some would be tempted to press such individuals into marriage—or even concubinage—to cure them. This would be a serious mistake, for without deep and successful psychotherapy first, they are truly not capable of a sexed relationship. Such a course would risk complicating the situation in the long run. It would also amount to treating marriage as therapy and the partner as a treatment, which seems a little revolting.

For some individuals, marriage could cause a reversal of their compensation of the neurosis. It is sufficient to recall the relatively frequent cases of ambivalent homosexuals who have been led into marriage. Dramatic consequences almost always follow, even including suicides.

Finally, the existence of positive celibates should demonstrate by itself the falsehood of the current implicit conviction that celibacy in itself causes or aggravates emotional disorder.

No one would deny that celibacy involves a frustration. The presence of another, dialogue, tenderness and its sexual expression, children—all these things respond to a spontaneous and fundamental human tendency. But although the nonrealization of the sexual tendency—in the broad sense—may cause suffering, it also may bring advantages.

Married life which binds each party in a continual response to the other-who-is-always-the-same can be very trying also. It establishes an interdependence which, although willed and loved, bears with it many limitations. A married man is no longer free to do what he pleases without taking account of his wife and children. Even on this level there are definite frustrations which are sometimes very vivid.

The man who gives up smoking his pipe because his wife cannot bear it does it out of love but suffers anyhow. A woman who had been an excellent pianist and deeply loved her music notices after a few years that she almost never plays any more because she has too much to do. She gets rusty and even loses some of the taste for her art, although the nostalgia lasts. One night, listening to a concert with her husband, tears may come furtively to her eyes when she remembers how much she loved her music.

Humanly speaking, it would be sheer stupidity to say that marriage is the only possible fulfillment and that celibacy leads to despair. It would be just as stupid as the contrary opinions of a St. Jerome who saw marriage as a kind of disgrace. Marriage is the most natural way to a certain kind of fulfillment. Celibacy can be a more unusual way to another kind. It all depends on what each person, according to his own personality and his resources for establishing positive relationships, will draw from the situation in which he is.

As a life situation, celibacy is not absurd; it can have positive meaning. Positive celibacy, as we have seen, means the possibility of establishing a network of relationships and activities through which the individual is fulfilled in himself and in participation with others. In negative celibacy the individual can *utilize* his situation in the same way, with or without psychological help according to the case.

In both cases it appears clear that the strongest motivation that gives the most complete meaning to celibacy is what we called the mystical motivation: the personal reference to the transsexual destiny of humanity in the world of the resurrection. It is important to realize that such a reference can be valid and consistent only if it is based on faith in Christ and does not get swallowed up in imaginary confusions and emotional compensations.

To most people celibacy means the absence of lived-out sex. The person who is celibate, in this view, is, therefore, continent. But this is not true. Celibacy is not directly concerned with the presence or absence of sexual activity. It is concerned with marriage. Anyone who is unmarried is perforce a celibate.

Marc Oraison in this book undertakes a vital psychological study of the celibate condition in its relation to sex. He does not consider the moral or spiritual values of celibacy; he is interested solely in the psychological significance of the celibate life in its varying manifestations.

Celibacy is either negative or positive, personal or institutional. Negatively celibate is the man who turns away from marriage either because he fears involving himself in the social commitment which it would require of him or because he is afraid of the opposite sex. Latently, at least, he is homosexual in his thinking and activity.

The positive celibate, on the other hand, is the person who actively chooses to be unmarried, not because he fears marriage and its social responsibilities but because he finds in celibacy the emotional, moral, and spiritual fulfillment he needs to be a mature human being. He is not a person alienated, by the fact of his interior celibacy, from the loves and sufferings of the people around him in the complex life of his community.

The major example of institutional celibacy is the Catholic priesthood. To be ordained a priest, one must first accept celibacy (and for the priest this means continence) as a necessary condition. Celibacy in this situation is an imposed legal obligation, not necessarily the response of the loving heart to the demands of God in his pilgrim people.

Although Oraison does not concern himself with the present controversy about priestly celibacy, he does underscore the fact that celibacy is the result of Church law, not the law of God.

We definitely need to think through anew our attitudes toward celibacy, particulary inasmuch as it involves the priesthood. This book furnishes us with the psychological data for this task. **$3.95**